TRAINER'S GUIDE

This document has been prepared for the National Literacy Secretariat by IME – Information Management & Economics, Inc.

Design: Jacques Anka, ANKA GRAPHIK

Plain Language: Clear and Simple – Trainer's Guide,
© Supply and Services Canada – 1994
Catalogue Number MP95-2/1-1994 E
ISBN 0-662-22420-5

TABLE OF CONTENTS

About This Guide v

Module 1: Introducing Plain Language 1
    What is plain language? 2
    Where did the term "plain language" come from? 3
    The importance of plain language in government 5
    Why do written communications break down? 7
    What is the plain language process? 9

Module 2: The Starting Point: Your Reader and Your Purpose 13
    The readers of a document 14
    The purpose of a document 16
    The impact of a document 17

Module 3: Organizing Your Ideas 19
    Introduction 20
    Principles of organizing information for the reader 21

Module 4: Using Appropriate Words 29
    Introduction 30
    Make your writing personal 32
    Use words with clear meanings 33
    Use words your reader will understand 34
    Use verbs rather than nouns 35
    Avoid or explain technical terms 41
    Avoid chains of nouns 44
    Avoid using acronyms 46

Avoid using jargon 47
Avoid using words from foreign languages 48
Use "may" and "can" correctly 48
Use "shall" correctly 49
Avoid gender reference, stereotypes and biased language 49

Module 5: Writing Clear and Effective Sentences 51
The sentence 52
Write in the active voice 53
Use a positive tone 56
One idea to a sentence 57
Write clear, direct and short sentences 60
Keep the sentence core together 62
Eliminate surplus words 65
Use adverbs and adjectives sparingly 67
Avoid unnecessary preambles 67
Eliminate double negatives 68
Eliminate prepositional phrases 69
Place modifiers correctly 70
Put parallel ideas in parallel constructions 71
Use point form and lists appropriately 73

Module 6: Writing Clear and Effective Paragraphs 75
The purpose of a paragraph 76
The structure of a paragraph 76
The use of transitions 78

Module 7: Presenting Your Message Effectively 81
    Text and readability 82
    Page format 85
    Headings and subheadings 86
    Highlighting 86
    Table of contents 87
    Visual effectiveness 87

Module 8: Testing and Revising the Document for Usability and Readability 89
    What is document testing? 90
    Why test a document? 90
    When should a document be tested? 91
    How to test a document for usability and readability 91
    What to do with the test results 99

Module 9: Putting It All Together: Working with Plain Language 101
    Analyzing the audience 102
    Writing for the reader 103
    Getting feedback 103

Plain Language Checklist

Material for Transparencies

Handouts

References

ABOUT THIS GUIDE

This guide provides a "framework" for people who lead training programs in a plain language approach to communication. Because it is impossible to teach a course the way another trainer would, you may wish to use this guide as a starting point for developing your own style and format.

The guide is based on a two-day course. While shorter courses can build awareness of the need for plain language, a longer course is needed to develop the technical skills necessary to apply the plain language approach in daily writing. A sample agenda for a two-day course is presented on page x.

A plain language approach involves understanding the needs of the readers, and then writing, revising and testing documents to make sure the documents meet those needs. The modules in this guide help participants build skills in these areas. However, it is the entire process that makes communication most effective. If participants are to develop the skills necessary to use a plain language approach, they need to work through all of the modules in this guide.

In a training setting, different participants have different needs. Some participants are more interested in documents for the general public, while others will have a specific interest in policy discussion papers or forms. You may be working with participants who deal with many types of communications. Our objective with the guide is to give you enough detail and background material so that you can "customize" the course for the different needs of participants and to match your own teaching style.

The guide is divided into nine modules. The first eight modules have been designed to take participants through the entire plain language process in steps so they can learn the techniques of a plain language approach to communication. The final module then gives participants a chance to work with all of the techniques at the same time.

Module 1 –

Introducing Plain Language introduces the concept of plain language and describes briefly what plain language is and what it is not. This module also gives a short history of the plain language movement as well as examples of the benefits of using plain language.

Module 2 –

The Starting Point: Your Reader and Your Purpose introduces the starting point of a plain language approach to communication – the reader. All plain language writing is reader focused and the module helps participants learn the techniques of analyzing the needs of different types of readers.

Module 3 –

Organizing Your Ideas presents techniques on how to organize information to meet the needs of the readers. The module presents ways of organizing information based on research into how people read and process information.

Module 4 –

Using Appropriate Words discusses how to simplify the choice of words and how to use words that make the reading of information easier and clearer.

Module 5 –

Writing Clear and Effective Sentences discusses how sentence structure and sentence length affect the reading and processing of information.

Module 6 –

Writing Clear and Effective Paragraphs examines how the structure of paragraphs can help readers process the information more effectively.

Module 7 –

Presenting Your Message Effectively examines the effect that text and page design have on reading. The module discusses techniques of text and page design that can make reading easier and improve comprehension.

Module 8 –

Testing and Revising the Document for Usability and Readability discusses how to test documents with readers to ensure that the document is effective. Because plain language is reader focused, it is essential to develop ways to bring the reader into the writing process and to get feedback from the reader. This module discusses techniques for testing and what the test results mean.

Module 9 –

Putting It All Together: Working with the Plain Language Process gives participants a chance to review and apply all of the techniques learned in modules 1–8.

A plain language approach to communication involves all of these steps. It is more than clear writing or effective design. An effective training program in plain language requires working through **all** of the modules in this guide in the order they are presented. In this way, participants can learn specific techniques for creating documents that are reader focused, clear, easy to read and effective.

There are eight types of material in this guide:
- text,
- examples,
- exercises,
- tips for trainers,
- overhead transparency masters,
- a checklist,
- handouts, and
- references.

The **text** develops the principles of a plain language approach. Each module begins with an "overview," "objectives" and "organization" of the module and then discusses the plain language principles for that module.

There is a wide range of **examples** throughout the guide to illustrate plain language principles. Most are taken from federal government publications. Participants learn best when they see examples from the types of documents they deal with every day.

Since learning comes mainly from doing, there are **exercises** at the end of modules 2 through 9 to give participants a chance to work with the concepts and techniques that are presented. Where appropriate, suggested solutions to the exercises have been included. The exercises are on separate sheets so you can photocopy them easily and use them as they are. You can also adapt them to your own style and your workshop participants.

The **tips for trainers** are based on the activities that have worked well in plain language workshops. They also try to anticipate questions that will come up.

Most of the examples in this guide are also included as **transparency masters** to be used in the workshops. You may want to adapt the overheads to each group of workshop participants. We have included more transparencies than are necessary for a two-day course so that you can choose which are appropriate to your presentation.

The **checklist** provides a reminder of plain language principles and a quick-reference tool for the participants to make sure they are being applied.

The **handouts** are made up of several word lists that appear in the guide and can serve as reference tools.

A list of **references** at the end of the guide contains sources for further information on writing and the plain language process.

Finally, this training guide is meant to complement the publication *Plain Language: Clear and Simple*. After the course, participants can use *Plain Language: Clear and Simple* as an effective reference tool that provides a summary of the key concepts developed in this training guide.

Whether you are new to plain language or familiar with this approach to communication, this guide contains the framework for developing and delivering an effective plain language course. We hope that you find it useful. Good luck!

PLAIN LANGUAGE: CLEAR AND SIMPLE

A Sample Two-day Agenda

Day 1

	9:00–9:10	Introduction and Overview
	9:10–9:30	Introduction to Plain Language
	9:30–10:30	The Starting Point: Your Reader and Your Purpose
	10:30–10:45	Break
	10:45–12:00	Organizing Information for Your Reader
	12:00–1:00	Lunch
	1:00–1:45	Using Appropriate Words
	1:45–2:30	Writing Clear and Effective Sentences (1) – Techniques
	2:30–2:45	Break
	2:45–3:30	Writing Clear and Effective Sentences (2) – Exercises
	3:30–4:00	Writing Clear and Effective Paragraphs

PLAIN LANGUAGE: CLEAR AND SIMPLE

A Sample Two-day Agenda, continued

Day 2

9:00–9:15	Review of Day 1. Preview of Day 2	
9:15–10:15	Presenting Your Message Effectively	
10:15–10:30	Break	
10:30–12:00	Testing	
12:00–1:00	Lunch	
1:00–1:45	Putting It All Together: Working with the Plain Language Process (Part 1 – Understanding the Reader)	
1:45–2:30	Putting It All Together: Working with the Plain Language Process (Part 2 – Organizing, Writing and Presenting the Information)	
2:30–2:45	Break	
2:45–3:45	Putting It All Together: Working with the Plain Language Process (Part 3 – Testing for Usability and Readability)	
3:45–4:00	Review and Evaluation	

MODULE 1

INTRODUCING PLAIN LANGUAGE

Overview

This module introduces participants to the concept of plain language. It describes what plain language is and what it is not. This module also gives a bit of the history behind the plain language movement as well as examples of the benefits of using plain language. It puts plain language in the context of the federal government's policy to use plain language to communicate more effectively and to improve service to the public. Finally, it describes the plain language process. This module complements material in chapter 1 of *Plain Language: Clear and Simple*.

Objectives

By the end of this module, participants will understand what is meant by the term "plain language" and how it differs from other forms of writing. Written communications are often the only contact people have with government. Participants will learn the importance and impact of the plain language process on these communications. Participants will understand the benefits of using plain language both for their readers and for their departments.

Organization

This module is organized into the following sections:
1. What is plain language?
2. Where did the term "plain language" come from?
3. The importance of plain language in government
4. Why do written communications break down?
5. What is the plain language process?

1. WHAT IS PLAIN LANGUAGE?

Plain language is an approach to communication that begins with the needs of the reader. When you use plain language, **what** you write is determined by your purposes for writing. **How** you write should be determined by your audience's reasons for reading and their reading skills.

Plain language matches the needs of the reader with your needs as a writer, resulting in effective and efficient communication. It is **effective** because the reader can understand the message. It is **efficient** because the reader can read and understand the message the first lime.

Unless you write clearly and directly, with the needs of your audience in mind, your readers may be left with more questions than answers. Difficult texts cause more:
- misunderstandings,
- errors,
- complaints,
- inquiries, and
- staff time lost to problem solving.

There are many misconceptions about plain language. Plain language is not a simplified style of writing. It involves more than replacing jargon and complex language with shorter sentences and familiar words. Plain language looks at the whole message – from the reader's point of view. Clear writing, effective organization and inviting presentation are all keys to creating readable, informative documents.

2. WHERE DID THE TERM "PLAIN LANGUAGE" COME FROM?

The term plain language has been in use in Canada since 1985, when the Canadian Legal Information Centre (CLIC) began its work to improve the clarity of legal and administrative writing. When CLIC was beginning its work, it looked to the experience of other countries in the world – specifically, the United Kingdom, the United States and Australia.

In the United Kingdom, the term "Plain English" had been used by the Plain English Campaign in its lobbying to improve access to social services. Later, the government of Margaret Thatcher adopted policies to make government communications more clear.

In the United States, President Carter initiated "paperwork" reduction in the mid-1970s and called on government to communicate more clearly with the public. In 1978, New York adopted the *Sullivan Act,* which was the first plain language law in the United States. Since then, ten states have adopted laws that require "plain language" in all consumer contracts. Another 30 states have laws that require clear language in rental agreements.

In Australia, the plain English movement developed after the Law Reform Commission of Victoria called for laws to be written in clear language. Since then, the government, law firms and the banking industry have been involved in numerous projects to improve the usability of legal documents and other types of written communications.

Canada has become a leader in the area of plain language. The federal government adopted a plain language policy for communications in 1988. The Treasury Board's communications policy is part of the Information and Administrative Management policy. The policy states:

5.1.2 Plain language

The obligation to inform the public includes the obligation to communicate effectively. Information about government policies, programs and services should be clear, objective and simple, and presented in a manner that is readily understandable. Messages should convey information relevant to public needs, use plain language and be expressed in a clear and consistent style.

Treasury Board Manual
90-10-01, p. 12

Since 1988, many federal government departments have been actively involved in plain language work. In 1990, an interdepartmental working group on plain language met to discuss ways to help encourage public servants to adopt a plain language approach to communication. The working group brought together representatives from 14 departments. It researched existing plain language materials and produced two guides on plain language – *Plain Language: Clear and Simple* and *Pour un style clair et simple*. The guides have been distributed to public servants including senior executives across government. In addition, more than 25,000 copies of the guides have been sold to the public, voluntary and business sectors as well as to educational institutions.

There have been other Canadian initiatives in the area of plain language. These include:

1. Three provinces (Alberta, Saskatchewan and Ontario) have adopted communications policies that require plain language to be used in all government communications.

2. In 1989, the Canadian Bar Association and the Canadian Bankers' Association Joint Committee on Plain Language recommended the use of plain language by lawyers and the financial services industry. These recommendations were later adopted by both organizations.

3. In 1991, Alberta became the first jurisdiction in Canada to adopt a plain language law – *the Financial Consumers Act*. The law requires certain consumer contracts to be written in "clear and easily understandable language."

3. THE IMPORTANCE OF PLAIN LANGUAGE IN GOVERNMENT

Three forces will shape government during the 1990s and into the next century – open government, improved service to the public and improved efficiency. Plain language is consistent with each of these goals.

In 1990, Statistics Canada surveyed Canadians between 16 and 69 years of age to determine how well they could read. The survey showed that 38% have difficulty with written materials. That means 38% of government clients have difficulty reading government information. A recent Decima survey found that 75% of Canadians felt that government information was too difficult to understand.

Formal writing often gives people the impression that government is distant and impersonal. Complex technical writing confuses and intimidates people and makes them feel removed from government. Plain language promotes open and honest communications that encourage the public to use government services and to understand the work of government on their behalf.

Governments today are committed to improving the services and programs they offer to the public. But this commitment comes at a time of budget restraint and escalating costs.

Organizations in both the private and public sectors have found that using plain language to improve their forms, letters and other documents has helped improve their services and saved time.

Although the costs of unclear communication can be difficult to determine, some reported examples of cost savings exist.

In Britain. Fifty thousand travellers every year fill out a Customs and Excise (C&E) form to claim lost luggage. 55% of the C&E forms had errors. Redesigning it brought the error rate down to 3%, saving staff 3,700 hours in processing. It cost the department about $3,500 to rewrite the form, but saved about $45,000 a year in processing costs.

In Ontario. The Ontario Human Rights Commission used to hand out copies of the Ontario Human Rights Code when anyone asked how to make a complaint. Then they produced plain language documents about the complaints process and basic information about the Human Rights Code. They estimate that they now save $15,000 per year in printing costs alone.

In Ontario. The Ministry of Colleges and Universities redesigned the application for the Ontario Student Assistance Program. The new application takes 50% less time to process. The program has been able to accomplish other work and improve customer service to students because of the staff time saved in processing the forms.

In British Columbia. The Ministry of the Attorney General implemented the Small Claims Court project to improve access to the court by ordinary citizens. Part of the project involved writing new legislation and rules of court using a plain language approach. They also redesigned all of the court forms and rewrote the brochures that explained court procedures. Since the new material was implemented, there has been a 40% increase in the number of cases. But, because there are fewer questions related to the forms and brochures, the Court Registry can handle the increased workload with the same number of staff as it had before the new forms were implemented.

4. WHY DO WRITTEN COMMUNICATIONS BREAK DOWN?

Written communications break down for two reasons:

1. Lack of feedback from the reader makes communicating difficult.

2. Written communications often attempt to reach people who do not share the same ethnic, professional or even organizational "culture."

Communication involves creating a common understanding. We communicate successfully when all people understand the message in the same way. The communication process is illustrated in the following diagram:

– Figure 1 –
The Communication Process

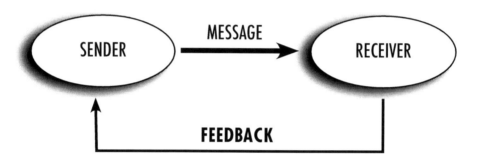

The message is used to try to create a common understanding. However, the critical component of this process is feedback. You can never be sure that the person receiving the message has the same understanding of that message unless you ask for their feedback.

When you communicate face-to-face, you rely on many types of feedback. You look at someone's eyes to see if they understand or at their body language to see if they are still interested. The difficulty with communicating through writing is that these types of feedback are not available. You send your written message to the other person and hope they develop the same understanding as you intended. Incorporating feedback into the writing process helps ensure that you communicate successfully.

The second reason written communications break down is that your reader does not share the same understanding of the subject or even the same interest in the subject. For example, public servants know a lot about the program in which they work – its history, its goals and objectives, and even its rules. However, people outside the department often do not have the same level of knowledge. In addition, every organization and profession develops its own language – special terms and abbreviations to help it work efficiently. People outside the organization or profession, however, may not understand this special language. Written communication often ignores the fact that the reader may not share the same understanding, language or "culture" as the writer. Plain language provides techniques for bridging this gap.

5. WHAT IS THE PLAIN LANGUAGE PROCESS?

Throughout this guide, we refer to plain language as a **process**. What we mean by this term is a sequence of steps that brings the reader into the writing process.

The plain language process begins with a clear understanding of the readers.

The next step is to communicate a message in a way that makes sense to the reader. This part of the process involves writing and revising. It also involves deciding how to present the message to support usability and readability. Layout and design affect even the most clearly written message.

Finally, the complete message – words and design – are "tested" with typical readers to see if the message is clear and easy to read and understand. Testing is an important way to get feedback from the reader and to help revise the document further to make sure that it is as effective as it can be.

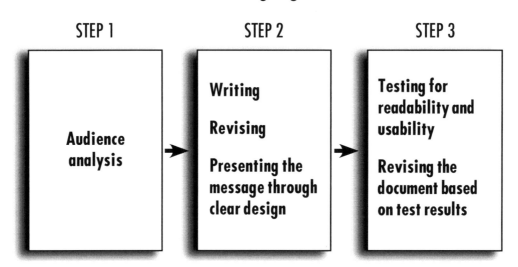

– Figure 2 –
The Plain Language Process

5.1 Audience analysis

The first step in the process is knowing who is receiving the document. Focus on your audience as individuals, not as a group of people:

- Who is going to read this document or fill out this form?
- Why are they using it?
- Where are they going to be when they use it?
- Will the situation be stressful or is the document likely to be intimidating?

TIP

YOU MAY BE ASKED...

Q. So far, plain language writing seems more like a course in communications than a course in writing. The Communications Sector in our department looks after communications. Why do I have to learn this?

A. We all need to be good communicators. Plain language writing is an approach to writing that helps us to make our writing clear and simple and more accessible to readers. Plain language writing is not a few rules on grammar and sentence structure. It is an attitude or approach to writing that will help you write better, no matter what type of document you are writing.

YOU MAY BE ASKED...

Q. How do I get information from a learners' group? What kinds of questions should I ask?

A. Many literacy workers have had some plain language experience, either attending a workshop or producing plain language material for learners. Explain your project to them and ask them if the material would be relevant to any of the learners in their group. Ask if it would be possible to include learners from the group in any testing of a document. Make sure that you send copies of the material to the literacy group when the project is finished. Literacy groups are always looking for written material to use as a resource.

If you are developing a document that will be used by new or unskilled readers, consult with a learners' group in the community. You can find out where the learners' groups are by looking in the yellow pages of your local telephone book under "Learn." These groups can help you understand what your readers really need to know rather than what you think they need to know.

Gathering data on existing documents or forms helps you determine how effective they have been with readers. Test an existing document with the intended audience. Find out the number and types of inquiries that have been made about it. Analyze the number and types of errors on forms that are processed, or the time it takes to process the form. These statistics help you to evaluate current problems or issues. They can also be very useful in evaluating the cost/benefits of plain language when the project is completed.

5.2 Writing, revising and designing

The second step in the process is creating the new document. This is where you match the needs of your reader with your purpose for writing the document. You should also analyze the needs of your department. The document must meet your systems, policy and operation requirements.

This stage of the process is the most time-consuming. Successive drafts must be reviewed and discussed, so allow enough time to design the document or form.

5.3 Testing

Testing your document is a critical part of the plain language process. After you have created a document which you think communicates effectively, you need to test it with the intended audience to make sure it works. Testing helps ensure that the document meets both the needs of your audience and your needs.

Avoid relying only on feedback from readers after the document is distributed. Test a document before the final draft.

After testing, revise the document based on the feedback. These revisions help to ensure an effective document.

MODULE 2

THE STARTING POINT: YOUR READER AND YOUR PURPOSE

Overview

This module introduces participants to the starting point of a plain language approach to communication – the reader. Participants need to understand the reader-oriented philosophy behind plain language writing. Once this concept is firmly in mind, they can use the techniques taught during the rest of the course. This module complements material in chapter 2 of *Plain Language: Clear and Simple*.

Objectives

By the end of this module, participants will understand the importance of their readers in the writing process. Participants will learn to begin every writing task by asking "Who will read this document?" and "Why will they be reading it?" Participants will learn the importance of identifying their purpose for writing a document. They will understand that the plain language process is based on matching the needs of the reader with the purpose of the document.

Organization

This module is organized into three sections:
1. The readers of a document
2. The purpose of a document
3. The impact of a document

1. THE READERS OF A DOCUMENT

Richard Saul Wurman, author of *Information Anxiety,* has written, "Communication equals remembering what it's like not to know."

Putting the readers' needs first can be hard when you are used to writing from your own perspective. The most important skill in developing a plain language approach is identifying your readers and being sensitive to their needs.

The focus on the reader is central to plain language writing. Everything from the tone you use to your choice of vocabulary, from document style to document testing and revision – flows from the belief that you must write for the reader.

> Every writer has a responsibility to present information in a way that is easy for the reader to understand. The reader should not have to struggle to figure out what the writer is trying to say.
>
> *Ruth Baldwin*
> *Clear Writing and Literacy, p. 2*

Plain language drafting is a form of writing that focuses on the needs of the reader. This style of drafting proceeds from the premise that, in written communication, it is the duty of the writer to make the effort to convey meaning to the reader.

Canadian Bar Association
The Decline and Fall of Gobbledygook, p. 1

TIP

YOU MAY BE ASKED...

Q. How can I find out more about my readers?

A. It may be possible to have telephone or in-person interviews with a few readers to gain a better understanding of their needs. Talk with staff who deal with the public. They'll know a lot about the public's information needs.

Spend time thinking about your readers and getting a feel for their situation and their needs.

Who is your intended audience? A document may have only one reader, for example, a supervisor, a colleague in another department or a member of the public.

A document may also have many readers. For example, they may be employees with different jobs who work together in a department, people who do the same type of work in a department, or the general public.

Your audience may be made up of readers of all ages or in the same age group. For example, a pamphlet to encourage students to stay in school might be for 13- to 16-year-olds. A booklet on what to do if a child turns to you after being sexually abused is for anyone a child would turn to – from a teenager to a grandparent.

Will the document be read by someone who is waiting in line for service? By someone who is emotionally upset? By someone who is annoyed by your department and is negative about its work? By someone who is very busy and always has too much to read?

Look at the characteristics that most of your readers share. For example, the key characteristic of readers of a pamphlet outlining the dangers of transporting zebra mussels to inland waters would be that they all use boats.

Decide on the most important audience for your document. People with properties on inland waters and environmentalists may be interested in the zebra mussels pamphlet too, but it is written to encourage boaters to take precautions. Boaters, therefore, are the primary audience for the information.

Do some research to find out more about your readers. When writing the pamphlet about zebra mussels, you might want to know what types of boats most commonly travel in the Great Lakes or inland waters. The Coast Guard or the people who run the locks on the Rideau Canal might be sources of this information. The boating registration system might provide some useful data.

An advantage of thinking about readers early on in the writing process is that it can help to clarify how you should distribute a document. The clearest and most accessibly written text is only useful if it finds its way to readers. By working out the target audience for a document, you can identify distribution strategies that may affect design, layout and the type of document you create. If you cannot send the pamphlet about zebra mussels to boaters because you cannot gel all the necessary addresses, you may want to think about getting the message across with a poster in boating supply stores and registration centres.

Your readers are probably less familiar with the subject than you are. Keep this in mind as you write. It will help you decide what the reader needs to know instead of what you want to write.

2. THE PURPOSE OF A DOCUMENT

Ask yourself why you are writing the document. What is your purpose?

Here are some examples of the purposes that documents can have:
- to **report** on discussions at a meeting,
- to **ask** someone to do something (such as provide information),
- to **inform** readers of a new policy,
- to **influence** a reader's actions, or
- to **explain** how to do something.

TIP

YOU MAY BE ASKED...

Q. My documents always seem to have more than one purpose – to inform, to influence, to get someone to do something and to keep as a record. It's all important. How do I pick which one is the most important?

A. Decide how the majority of your audience will use your document. This will dictate its purpose. If there are a number of different audiences for a document, and each is large enough, consider creating more than one type of document: a brochure for those wanting a brief overview of a new program; a more detailed booklet for those who want to access the program; and a step-by-step guide for those who are completing the necessary paperwork.

Q. When I write to the public, my job is to make the government look good. I have been told that that is always my primary purpose.

A. The government looks good when it gives clear and direct information to the public. Platitudes about how good a policy is don't help people who want to know how the policy affects them and what they should do. In this case, your purpose is to inform the public about the policy.

TIP

YOU MAY BE ASKED...

Q. My audience for this document is just too diverse. It is impossible to figure out the audience characteristics – I have to write for the general public.

A. Advertisers and pollsters know that no one is the "general public." They study their audience carefully to decide how to get their message across or how to analyze survey results. Writers also have to identify who their readers are and what their reasons for reading are if they want to be effective communicators. Test a document before publication to make sure that your purpose for writing matches the audience's reasons for reading. Before writing, talk to colleagues who deal directly with the public. Keep track of the number and types of requests for information. All these things will help you identify your audience and ensure efficient and effective communication.

Q. I am writing a letter to a member of the public but my supervisor has to review it before I send it. Who is my audience?

A. You need to write to meet the needs of the person to whom you are sending the letter. However, you may want to talk to your supervisor about the approach you took in your letter.

Q. I never write anything for people outside the government. Most of what you are talking about seems to be for documents that are meant for the general public. My writing is all for people just like me.

A. It is true that writing for the public is a special challenge, but plain language writing skills will work for you even when you are writing memos to your supervisor or to others in your department. You still need to think about how to make sure that your message is clear.

You may find it hard to single out one purpose. But a document with one primary focus is more likely to communicate its message effectively.

Knowing the primary purpose of a document helps you determine the:
- key readers of the document,
- essential information to include,
- order in which to present the information,
- length,
- tone (neutral, friendly or assertive),
- style (question and answer, narrative or point form),
- format (pamphlet, booklet, letter or poster),
- design (type size, headings or illustrations), and
- urgency of completing the writing task.

3. THE IMPACT OF A DOCUMENT

Once you have decided who the audience is and what your purpose is, think about what effect you want your document to have on the reader.

Is the reader supposed to do something after reading the document? For example, do you want the reader to come to a meeting with certain information?

Is the reader supposed to remember certain information? For example, do you want the reader to know how to clean a boat properly before moving it from one of the Great Lakes?

Is the reader supposed to agree with your point of view? For example, do you want to convince the reader that a change in policy is necessary?

Is the reader supposed to keep the document and use it as a reference? For example, do you want to provide the reader with a manual explaining how to access information in an office computer system?

The answer to the question – What do you want your reader to do? – affects how you present information. If the reader is supposed to come to a meeting, for example, then the date and time of the meeting might be the first thing to put in the document. Information about the agenda, the other participants and the documents to bring along might be of secondary importance.

The three questions – Who is your audience? Why are you writing this document? What do you want your reader to do? – help you focus on the reader's needs, your own purpose and the intended impact of the document. Incorporating the answers to these questions in the writing process ensures effective and efficient communication.

EXERCISE

WHO IS YOUR READER?

Pick a new writing sample from the group or department or use the letter in Exercise #3 of this module.

Ask the group about the document's audience. Talk about their ideas. Discuss how the document's audience affected the way the document was written and how the information was presented. Ask participants to suggest ways they might improve the document now that they have thought about its readers.

EXERCISE

THINKING ABOUT YOUR READER

Discuss the following scenario with the group:

> Their department has been undergoing some reorganization. Some people in their sector will be moving to another sector. Some new people from another department will be joining their sector. They have been asked to write a note to staff explaining these changes.

What are the characteristics of their readers?

How will this affect what they write?

EXERCISE

THE PURPOSE OF A DOCUMENT

Read the following section of a letter sent home by a child's teacher:

> At times, your child will bring home a book she/he can read. Please receive this sharing with respect and without judgment. This is not the time to interrupt, or to correct the reading unless your child seeks help. This is not the time to make your child sound out unknown words – that type of reading approach may not be the right one for your child at this time. Any concerns you have about reading performance should be addressed to me immediately. Please do not burden your six-year-old with the responsibility of having to explain my educational practices. If I sound very overprotective, you are right. It is very hard work teaching children to read so they always love it – it takes only one harsh word to make that learning seem worthless.

This is a paragraph from a letter sent to parents by a principal of a private school. Tell the group that the parents' committee has asked them to rewrite it. What would they do first?

MODULE 3

ORGANIZING YOUR IDEAS

Overview

This module discusses five principles of organizing information for the reader. This module complements material in chapters 2 and 3 of *Plain Language: Clear and Simple*.

Objectives

By the end of this module, participants will understand how clear writing is a product of clear thinking. They will understand that by planning a document's contents before they write, they will spend less time writing and rewriting. Participants will learn five ways of organizing information and the impact of each method on the reader.

Organization

This module is organized into two sections:
1. Introduction
2. Principles of organizing information for the reader:
   - organize the information logically,
   - orient your reader to the text,
   - put the most important information first,
   - help your readers find information, and
   - put all the information about a specific subject in one place.

1. INTRODUCTION

Give your readers what they need. Editor William Zinsser says, "if the reader is lost, it is generally because the writer has not been careful enough to keep him on the path."

Clear, organized thinking produces clear, logical writing. If your thinking and your writing are badly organized, your message – and your readers – will be lost. You can solve some communications problems by changing words or sentence structure. Other problems involve the way words or thoughts are arranged. You can fix these only by thinking carefully about the content of your message and the organization of your document – from your reader's point of view.

What you are writing about is familiar to you. You know the specialized vocabulary of the subject. Your readers are probably less familiar with the subject. If their level of understanding is significantly different than yours, they think very differently about the subject. In this situation, it's easy to emphasize information that is not relevant to your readers, or to omit information that they need.

The organization of your document is an essential part of conveying your message clearly.

TIP

This module is critical to the plain language approach. Most writers organize their writing from their own point of view. This module asks participants to organize information from the reader's point of view.

2. PRINCIPLES OF ORGANIZING INFORMATION FOR THE READER

Information needs to be organized according to what the readers need to know and how they will be using the document.

Complex information is more understandable when it is divided into manageable, logical segments. People read more quickly, solve problems faster and recall information more accurately when information is presented in "manageable chunks." The definition of manageable chunks depends on the nature of the information and the characteristics of the audience.

2.1 Organize the information logically

The ideas in your document must be presented logically. Just as important, that logic must be clear to your readers. Therefore, include a good table of contents. As well, clear headings throughout the document help readers see the organization and flow of information. Headings also guide readers through the text and help readers anticipate information. They provide quick access to the information a reader needs. These two techniques (table of contents and headings) are discussed in greater detail later. In shorter documents, you may want to explain how you have organized the information in an "Introduction" to the document instead of using a table of contents.

There are many ways to organize information. Here are a few:
- from general to specific or specific to general,
- from most important to least important,
- from positive to negative, and
- step by step.

Organizing information from the general to the specific works well when the reader needs the "big picture" before dealing with more specific information. However, sometimes the "big picture" is too complex for most readers to deal with. For example, if the big picture is the legislation that governs a program, it is probably something too complex for people to relate to. In this case, it may be better to begin with the specific and let the general information follow.

Organizing information from the most important to the least important works well when you have readers that are looking for something specific. For example, if the document title asks a question (or if you know the reader has a specific question in mind when reading the document), the most important information for the reader is the answer. The answer should be first, followed by an explanation.

Organizing information from the positive to the negative gives readers a chance to deal with what can be done before dealing with exclusions and exceptions. If the document is organized in this way, it is important to tell readers they must read the whole thing so they don't stop after reading the positive and miss the important negative information.

If the document is explaining a procedure, many readers find a step-by-step organization helpful. For example, if applying for citizenship, the reader is likely to want to know what the procedure is and how long it will take. In this case, organizing the information according to the steps that the applicant must complete would be helpful. Chronological order is another form of step-by-step organization. It may be the most logical approach for describing procedures or a sequence of events.

2.1.1 Organizing documents that give instructions.

Documents that give instructions should begin by telling readers what you want them to do. You can tell them why they must pay attention to your instructions or why you are asking them to do something.

Then you should state any qualifiers or conditions to the instructions (who does what, what can or cannot be done, when to do it, why it is important). You should also include any other information that your readers need in order to comply with your instructions. If your readers must agree to something they do not really understand, they may feel anxious and resentful.

The document should end with the consequences of failing to comply. Your readers need to know what's going to happen to them if they don't follow your instructions. Tell them clearly and directly, without any irrelevant or threatening details.

2.1.2 Organizing letters and memos.

Even though letters are predominantly for external use and memos, including those on e-mail, are for internal use, the following organization guidelines apply to both.

State clearly your reason for writing. Make sure that readers know if you're writing to inform them or to ask them to do something.

If you are writing for more than one reason, state your full agenda in the first paragraph. For example, "I am writing to provide information about the committee's activities to date and to request your help in preparing for the next meeting."

Then you should identify issues clearly and present recommendations, options or requests in a sequence that makes sense to your readers.

End by summarizing your recommendations or conclusions. You can also end with an "action list." This type of ending is common in letters and memos. It summarizes who is responsible for doing what, and when and where it must be done.

2.1.3 Developing a logical flow.

Your readers should be able to move easily through the text without losing their train of thought. Your document should flow logically from beginning to end, and within each section and paragraph. Remember that your readers are probably less familiar with your subject than you are. Always begin with what your readers are likely to know, and progress to new or difficult concepts. Do this with paragraphs and with your whole document.

If your readers know almost nothing about the subject, periodically summarize the main points you have made before going on to new information. It helps them become familiar with the information.

2.2 Orient your reader to the text

When readers pick up a document and begin to read it, they need to put the document into context. They need to understand what it is they are about to read, how the document is organized, and what the purpose is of the information they are about to read.

Here is an example of how to orient the reader:

EXAMPLE

> Unemployment Insurance (UI) protects you when you lose your job. It provides temporary income while you look for another job, or are sick, pregnant or caring for a newborn or adopted child.
>
> Most Canadians work in jobs covered by UI. This means they pay into the UI system and collect benefits when they are out of work.
>
> This booklet is designed to help you understand the process involved in applying for Unemployment Insurance. It will explain what procedures to follow, list some of the documents you need, as well as go over your rights and responsibilities.
>
> *Employment and Immigration Canada*
> *A Worker's Guide to Unemployment Insurance*

This example puts the booklet into context. It tells the reader what UI is and why the booklet was written.

2.3 Put the most important information first

Readers expect a document to be relevant. Your document's beginning should help your readers anticipate the document's content. If they do not see what they are most interested in, then they are likely to lose interest.

For example, a brochure entitled "How to Prove You Are a Canadian Citizen" begins with the following information:

> With the *Canadian Citizenship Act* of 1947, Canada became the first Commonwealth country to have its own citizenship. "Canadian" became an official citizenship status. Many other countries have modelled their citizenship laws on ours.
>
> A citizen of Canada, whether by birth or by naturalization, enjoys all the rights and freedoms outlined in the Canadian Constitution. Among them are:
> - full political participation...
> - foreign travel and freedom to return...
> - full economic right...
>
> *Multiculturalism and Citizenship Canada*
> *How to Prove You Are a Canadian Citizen*

In this case, the title of the brochure raises a question. What the reader needs to know is the answer – how to prove it. The information at the beginning neither answers the questions nor provides an overview of the answer.

The brochure could begin with the most important information – the answer to the question. For example, it could begin with the following:

> There are two ways to prove you are a Canadian citizen...

Then, the brochure could include background information on what Canadian citizenship is.

2.4 Help your readers find information

Many documents are not read from start to finish, but used to check specific information. For example, policies and procedures are rarely read from start to finish. In this case, the material needs to be organized in a way that makes it easy to find information.

The best way to accomplish this is by using headings and subheadings to break up the text. Current research on how people read and use written information shows that they find complex information more understandable when you divide it into manageable chunks. People can read more quickly, solve problems faster and recall information more accurately.

Headings are easy for your reader to remember and use for quick reference later. They are especially useful in guiding your readers through the middle of your document where the bulk of the information is found.

Headings should be precise and progress logically. Precise headings help readers by allowing them to locate the information they need or skim over sections they know do not apply to them. They should progress logically from the general to the specific, or from the beginning to the end. Your headings should accurately describe the text that follows.

2.4.1 Add examples to clarify or illustrate.

Does your document contain complex concepts or procedures? Examples help to make them seem real and relevant to your readers. They demonstrate how information can apply in a practical situation.

When selecting examples, remember to include people and situations your readers can relate to. This means including women, senior citizens, persons with disabilities, people of various economic means, people in non-traditional occupations and people from a variety of ethnic and cultural backgrounds.

Make sure that examples relate directly to the information you are trying to convey. To identify examples, use a subheading or an introductory phrase like "for example" or "for instance."

2.5 Put all the information about a specific subject in one place

Readers do not like having to look in many places to read about a particular topic. Documents with many cross-references are frustrating to use. If possible, put all the information about a particular topic or idea in one place. If this cannot be done, make sure that cross-references are clear and used only when absolutely necessary.

EXERCISE

ORGANIZING INFORMATION FOR THE READER

Use a range of documents from the participants' program area or other appropriate documents. It is important that the documents not be too long because participants will have to deal with all of the information in each document.

Ask participants to read the documents and determine if:
- the information in each is organized logically,
- the information is organized from the readers' point of view,
- the documents orient the reader,
- the most important information is put first, or
- the information is broken up into manageable chunks with effective headings and subheadings.

Ask participants to choose which documents are well-organized and which need reorganization. For the latter, ask participants to develop headings for the documents and list information that would be included under each heading. What information would they put first? What information would not be included? Is there any information that is not in the document that should be?

Let participants work individually for about 10–15 minutes. Then, let small groups compare and discuss their organization. Ask each group to report back to the large group by putting their headings and/or outline on a flip chart. Each group should justify why they organized the information the way they did. Let the full group discuss the results.

EXERCISE #2   MODULE 3

EXERCISE

ORGANIZING INFORMATION FOR THE READER

Use the following scenario for this exercise.

> You have just come from a staff meeting at which people had a heated discussion about some office management problems. You were asked to write a memo to your supervisor right away, telling her about the problems and asking her to come to a meeting with the group. You had some ideas about how the problems could be solved but the other people at the meeting didn't agree with you. You are worried that your supervisor will feel that your group is ganging up against her and that she will come to the meeting angry. You promised to circulate the note to everyone who attended the meeting.

How will you organize the information in the memo?

Will your readers understand your organization and what the memo's purpose is?

PLAIN LANGUAGE **CLEAR** AND **SIMPLE**

MODULE 4

USING APPROPRIATE WORDS

Overview

This module presents the role that words play in a plain language approach to communication. It addresses a number of principles related to the use of clear language in writing. This module complements material in chapter 5 of *Plain Language: Clear and Simple*.

Objectives

By the end of this module, participants will understand the importance of choosing words that make sense to their readers, and words that convey their message clearly and accurately. They will learn the importance of seeing their choice of words from their readers' point of view. Participants will understand that the tone of their document directly affects how their message will be received, that "how" they write is just as important as "what" they write.

Organization

This module is organized into the following sections:
1. Introduction
2. Make your writing personal
3. Use words with clear meanings
4. Use words your reader will understand
5. Use verbs rather than nouns

6. Avoid or explain technical terms
7. Avoid chains of nouns
8. Avoid using acronyms
9. Avoid using jargon
10. Avoid using words from foreign languages
11. Use "may" and "can" correctly
12. Use "shall" correctly
13. Avoid gender reference, stereotypes and biased language

1. INTRODUCTION

Words are symbols for what we perceive with our senses. They communicate what we think, feel and do. We must agree on the basic meaning and use of a word in order for it to be useful for us in communicating with one another. The more complex the idea or thought, the more difficult it is to express it precisely in words.

Many people associate plain language with simple words. This is inconsistent with the plain language approach used in this guide. Many things can become barriers to comprehension. Words are just one potential barrier.

Language involves a group of people associating the same meaning with the same set of symbols. When the writer and the reader have very different experiences, they are likely to associate very different meanings with the same word.

Consider the word "horse." What comes to mind when you think of the word horse? Some people might picture the black stallion of recent movies, a powerful sleek horse rearing high. Someone else might recall from childhood the sensation of straddling a fat, rough-haired pony. Another person might think with distaste of the never-ending chore of cleaning the horse stalls in an uncle's barn.

The way people interpret a word is influenced by their personal backgrounds, education and social experiences. As a result, communicating accurately with written words is difficult even when concrete things, like "horse," are involved. It is even more difficult with official writing, which is concerned with explaining or discussing more abstract concepts – regulations, policies, procedures, responsibilities and rights.

Another potential barrier is writing style. How you say something to your readers is just as important as what you say. Your writing style is like the tone of your voice. It conveys a sense of what you think about both the subject matter and your readers. It also forms the basis of how your readers perceive you or your organization.

Your writing style is based on your choice of words and the way that you combine them in sentences and paragraphs. For example, "police officer" is a neutral or respectful term. "Officer of the law" is an exaggerated, formal expression. The word "policeman" may reveal a gender bias. "Cop" has a negative connotation, and "pig" is clearly derogatory.

The tone of your writing influences how your readers understand and respond to your message. A tone that is patronizing, negative, authoritarian, legalistic or bureaucratic will make your readers uncomfortable. A formal, impersonal tone can alienate or intimidate, while a colloquial or casual tone can sometimes make your message seem unimportant or unreliable.

As someone who writes government documents, you need to be aware of the differences between you and your readers. See your choice of words from their point of view.

2. MAKE YOUR WRITING PERSONAL

People respond to other people, not to bureaucratic structures. If you use a friendly, conversational tone when writing for the general public, your documents and your organization will seem more approachable and accessible.

Address your readers directly. Don't talk about them indirectly in the third person or by using labels such as "employees," "employers," "clients" or "citizens."

Good Examples of Making Your Writing Personal

It is difficult to make changes alone. We all learn by listening and sharing our ideas with other people. People need to let others know their thoughts. You can do this by reading and writing letters to newspapers. You can go to meetings to hear speakers. You can ask questions and make suggestions. You can discuss ideas in groups at your children's schools and in your neighbourhood. All people can help to make Canada a better place. Sharing with others makes our own lives more interesting and helps us work for a better Canada.

Multiculturalism and Citizenship Canada
The Canadian Citizen, 1985, p. 3

If You Suspect Sexual Abuse

The best way to respond to a child who you suspect may have been sexually abused is to listen carefully to what the child says and to be attentive to his or her behaviour. Show your concern. Ask if anything is the matter. But do not press for an answer. Let the child know that you are ready to listen at any time.

Department of Justice Canada
What to do if a child tells you of sexual abuse, 1989, p. 3

3. USE WORDS WITH CLEAR MEANINGS

The meaning of words is not fixed. Definitions change over time. Regional and cultural variations in the use of words are common. People are constantly inventing new words or meanings in their work and their recreational activities. All these changes in language make it difficult to find good, clearly defined words with which to express your thoughts accurately.

The employee co-ordinates selected horizontal administrative activities and acts as a functional co-ordinator for cross-sectoral development initiatives…

Ad for Senior Project Officer position

Vague words like "process" and "system" are often used in writing and speech without being defined. One dictionary's definition of "system," for example, includes such varied meanings as:
- a regularly interacting group of items,
- an organized set of ideas intended to explain the workings of a whole,
- an established procedure, and
- a harmonious arrangement.

What comes to mind when you read the word "system?" A psychologist might assume it refers to interactions among members of a family. A person familiar with computers might think of computer hardware, or maybe a bulletin board service.

4. USE WORDS YOUR READER WILL UNDERSTAND

The language you use depends on the audience you are addressing. If you are writing for doctors, you can use terms like "myocardial infarction." But if you are writing primarily for a more diverse audience, you must be an interpreter as well as a writer.

When you write for the general public, you must take readers who know little or nothing about your subject and lead them step by step to an understanding of it. Remember their reasons for reading as well as your reasons for writing. Explain your concepts and terms in words that your readers understand.

Use simple, everyday words where possible. Readers become tired and discouraged when faced with a text full of unfamiliar words and expressions.

TIP

YOU MAY BE TOLD...

These words sound too simple. I don't want to write using street talk. I like writing that has some style.

A. What we are talking about here is using words that are appropriate. It is not that the words on the left should never be used. However, the point is that we tend to overuse these words.

Here are some examples of words that can often substitute for multi-syllable words:

Instead of:	Use:
accomplish	do
ascertain	find out
disseminate	send out, distribute
endeavour	try
expedite	hasten, speed up
facilitate	work out, devise, form
in lieu of	instead of
locality	place
optimum	best, greatest, most
strategize	plan
utilize	use

5. USE VERBS RATHER THAN NOUNS

Verbs are "do" words. Nouns are "thing" words. Verbs express action better than nouns. Here's a simple, direct sentence that tells the reader to do something:

You should apply the techniques of plain language every day.

Let's make one small change in the sentence by turning the verb "apply" into the noun "application." Look what happens to the sentence.

You should application the techniques of plain language every day.

It is no longer a sentence. It does not make sense. In order to communicate the message contained in the original sentence, we must add words.

> You should practise the application of the techniques of plain language every day.

Here's what happened:

1. We added another verb, "practise," to replace the one we changed into a noun.

2. We added the article "the" to separate the new verb "practise" from the noun "application."

3. We added the preposition "of" as a glue word because "techniques" was bumped as the object of the verb when "application" took its place.

Nouns like "application" – nouns that are derived from verbs – are known as nominalizations or derivative nouns. Government, legal and business material are full of them. Nominalizations are impersonal and often vague. Nominalizations prevent the reader from imagining someone performing a task. Often, you can spot these derivative nouns by their common endings: -ance, -ancy, -ant, -ence, -ency, -ent, -ion, -ment, -tion, -y.

Most of what you write is intended to tell your readers what they must do, or what they are permitted to do. Since you are telling them what action to take, use action verbs. When you write a noun that is derived from a verb, see if you can turn it back into a verb.

Here are examples of nominalizations and suggested revisions:

Establishment of goals for the hiring, training and promotion of designated group employees. Such goals will consider projections for hiring, promotions, terminations, lay-offs, recalls, retirements and, where possible, the projected availability of qualified designated group members.

Employment and Immigration Canada
Federal Contractors Program, 1991, p. 5

Revised

Establish goals for hiring, training and promoting employees from designated groups. Such goals will reflect the rate at which we will hire, promote, terminate, lay off or recall members of designated groups and the rate at which they will retire. Where possible, the goals will project how many qualified members will be available.

EXAMPLE

Factor Music Action Canada assist in the creation, production and syndication of new radio programs by private Canadian production companies for future broadcast by radio stations in Canada.

Communications Canada
Sound Recording Development Program Information Guide, 1986, p. 15

Revised

Factor Music Action Canada will assist private Canadian production companies to create, produce and syndicate new radio programs for future broadcast by radio stations in Canada.

EXAMPLE

Improvement of the Defence Planning and Force Development process is a prerequisite to improvement of the Defence Program Management System.

Auditor General of Canada
Report of the Auditor General, 1992, p. 17

Revised

We need to improve the Defence Planning and Force Development process before we can improve the Defence Program Management System.

> **EXAMPLE**

Such immigrant communities may well become targets for penetration, manipulation and coercion by foreign intelligence services, thus threatening to limit expression of their new-found rights.

Canadian Security Intelligence Service Public Report, 1992

Revised

Foreign intelligence services may well penetrate, manipulate and coerce such immigrant communities, thus threatening to limit expression of their new-found rights.

> **EXAMPLE**

Communication by the organization's chief executive officer to employees, unions and/or employee associations of the commitment to achieve equality in employment through the design and implementation of an employment equity plan.

*Employment and Immigration Canada
Federal Contractors Program, 1991, p. 3*

Revised

Communication by the chief executive officer to employees, unions and/or employee organizations that the organization is committed to achieving equality in employment by designing and implementing an employment equity plan.

Here is a list of derivative nouns that are commonly used and a list of the preferred verb forms.

Derivative noun	Verb form
acceptance	accept
application	apply
approval	approve
assumption	assume
calculation	calculate
certification	certify
complaint	complain
conservation	conserve
consideration	consider
contribution	contribute
decision	decide
deduction	deduce
delivery	deliver
designation	designate (name, appoint)
deterioration	deteriorate
determination	determine
disclosure	disclose
discovery	discover
disposal, disposition	dispose (sell, give away)
distribution	distribute
education	educate
enforcement	enforce
examination	examine
filing	file
inclusion	include
information	inform
investigation	investigate
movement	move

TIP

YOU MAY BE TOLD...

I have to use technical language. My area deals with very specialized knowledge and very complicated legislation.

A. When you need to use technical language, use it. But, if the reader does not understand you, you have not achieved your goal of communication. Technical words should be explained in the text by either a definition or an example if there is even a remote chance that the reader may not understand.

Derivative noun (cont'd)	Verb form (cont'd)
objection	object
payment	pay
persistence	persist
prevention	prevent
promotion	promote
qualification	qualify
reaction	react
receipt	receive
recurrence	recur
reduction	reduce
reliance	rely
remittance	remit
residence	reside
resistance	resist
specification	specify
statement	state
submission	submit

6. AVOID OR EXPLAIN TECHNICAL TERMS

Whenever possible, avoid words that your readers do not know. Every occupation and interest group has special terms. These terms become a problem only when you can't distinguish between terms that are necessary working tools and terms that are jargon.

While it is generally better to try to avoid technical terms, this cannot always be done. If you must use a technical term, explain it. There are two general ways to explain technical terms – by giving a definition of the technical term, or by giving an example.

Definitions should contain words that are unambiguous and are likely to be known by the reader, or synonyms or derivatives for the term you are defining. They should use positive, precise language.

Here are examples of how technical terms are defined and suggested revisions:

EXAMPLE

Spousal registered retirement income fund – A spousal RRIF is an RRIF under which your spouse is the annuitant that has received funds from a spousal RRSP or another spousal RRIF.

Revenue Canada
Pensions – An RRSP Tax Guide, 1991, p. 7

Revised

A spousal registered retirement income fund is a reserve which pays yearly to your spouse and which has received money from a spousal RRSP or another spousal RRIF.

EXAMPLE

Economic espionage may be defined as the illegal or clandestine acquisition of critical Canadian economic information and technology by foreign governments or their surrogates.

Canadian Security Intelligence Service Public Report, 1992

Revised

Economic espionage means foreign governments or their agents obtaining critical Canadian economic and technological secrets illegally.

If it is not possible to define the term simply and remain accurate, use an example to give the reader an idea of what the technical term means. With complex material, the only way to make a point clearly may be to use an example. Examples work well to show how abstract information applies in a practical situation.

Examples may be short and simple, or long and detailed. Short examples may be included in the main text, or set off from it in some way. Long examples should always be set off from the text.

When selecting examples, remember to include people and situations that your readers can relate to.

7. AVOID CHAINS OF NOUNS

Chains of nouns are two or more nouns used to name one thing. They are often difficult for a reader to understand and give a bureaucratic tone to documents. You may have encountered expressions like the following:
- resource allocation procedures,
- transport facility development programming,
- consumer information-seeking behaviour, and
- product extension mergers.

The difficulty with noun chains is that one of the nouns serves the function of a noun. The other words in the string serve as adjectives or adverbs for the noun.

Here are examples of noun chains and suggested revisions:

Registered retirement savings plan deduction limit

Revised

Maximum amount you can deduct for contributions to your registered retirement savings plan

EXAMPLE

Registered retirement savings plan dollar limit

Revised

Maximum amount you can contribute to your registered retirement savings plan

EXAMPLE

Unused registered retirement savings plan deduction room

Revised

Unused portion of the maximum amount you can deduct for contributions to your registered retirement savings plan

Revenue Canada
Pensions – An RRSP Tax Guide, 1991, p. 7

8. AVOID USING ACRONYMS

The name of an organization or program is often identified by an acronym – an abbreviation consisting of the first letter of each word in the name, for example, RCMP. Don't assume that your readers know what the acronym refers to. Write out the full name the first time you use it, and put the acronym next to it in brackets. You can then use the acronym in your text. Be careful not to use too many acronyms though. Your readers will soon be lost in a sea of ADMs, DOCs or RFPs.

Here are examples of acronyms and suggested revisions:

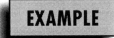

If you earn benefits for 1991 under an RPP benefit provision or under a DPSP, your employer normally has to calculate and report a 1991 PA for you.

Revenue Canada
Pensions – An RRSP Tax Guide, 1991, p. 9

Revised

If you earn benefits for 1991 under a Registered Pension Plan benefit provision or under a Deferred Profit-Sharing Plan, your employer normally has to calculate and report a 1991 Pension Adjustment for you.

TIP

Technically, many of these are not acronyms, but abbreviations. However, more and more people are calling any abbreviation that is derived from the first letter of words an acronym.

EXAMPLE

A DNA sex probe was developed at DFO's PBS, W. Vancouver Laboratory, in conjunction with Sea Spring Salmon Farm and the Science Council of B.C.

Fisheries and Oceans Canada
Partnership in Success, 1992

Revised

A DNA sex probe was developed at the Department of Fisheries and Ocean's Pacific Biological Station, West Vancouver Laboratory, in conjunction with Sea Spring Salmon Farm and the Science Council of British Columbia.

9. AVOID USING JARGON

Will all your words be understood by people outside of your workplace? Avoid using a term such as "vertical federalism" in a paper that you distribute to the public unless you explain it clearly in the text. But if you have to explain a term, consider using an alternate expression from the start.

Trendy, fashionable expressions, such as "level playing field," "downtime," "leading edge," "streamline," "interface with" and "rationalization of resources" are used far too often. They can undermine the impact of what you're trying to say because they are not well understood by the public.

10. AVOID USING WORDS FROM FOREIGN LANGUAGES

If you are producing an English-language document, write in English. Scattering your writing with expressions borrowed from another language only confuses your readers. Avoid even common Latin abbreviations like e.g. and i.e.

Here is a list of commonly found Latin expressions and their English equivalents:

ad infinitum	endlessly
bona fide	genuine, sincere
nota bene	please note
e.g.	for example
i.e.	that is
per annum	per year

11. USE "MAY" AND "CAN" CORRECTLY

Readers often find the use of the verb forms "may" and "can" confusing.

"May" covers two very different social meanings. It is used to express a conditional choice (You may want to wait…) or give permission (You may seek the advice…)

"Can" has a broader spectrum of meanings and a more conversational tone.

To avoid confusion, use "can" if the conditional choice is the message. If permission is the message, use phrases such as "you are allowed to," "government regulations permit" or "we let you."

12. USE "SHALL" CORRECTLY

"Shall" is a verb that creates confusion. "Shall" can denote either obligation or future tense.

If obligation is the message, use "must." If the future tense is the message, use "will."

13. AVOID GENDER REFERENCE, STEREOTYPES AND BIASED LANGUAGE

Effective writing is gender neutral and free of bias. Bias in writing is a product of the words you choose and the attitudes they represent. For example, referring to the "girl on the reception desk" suggests that the receptionist, whatever her age, is immature and perhaps not to be taken seriously. Describing someone as "confined to a wheelchair" victimizes the person. A wheelchair is not confining. It provides mobility for persons who cannot walk.

Avoid mentioning gender, race, age or disability when it is not pertinent. Use gender-neutral terms. Be sensitive to language that may reinforce stereotypes or patronize or demean a particular group, race or sex. For example, use "persons with disabilities" instead of "handicapped." Avoid clichés such as "an old-maid attitude" or "the man in the street."

EXERCISES

USING APPROPRIATE WORDS

Have participants work on one or more of the following texts. For each, ask them to circle words they think would create problems for readers. Then, ask them to write the sentence using the principles of clear language in this module.

1. Universal education and the imperatives of the shifting techno-economic order have eliminated reading (and writing) as the exclusive tools and intellectual property of the literati.

2. It is quite startling to note Canadians' apparent zest for pleasure reading – particularly in light of the collective angst about the sorry state of reading in our putatively post-literate society.

3. "Bias" has been defined as an inclination towards a specific attitude or preconceived opinion about certain groups of people or things. A "stereotype" represents a widespread view of a particular group which does not take into consideration intrinsic, individual characteristics. In applying the guidelines, material should be reviewed for words, images and situations that reinforce erroneous perceptions or suggest that all or most members of a racial or ethnic group are the same.

4. Prior to completing the application the applicants should determine if their qualifications meet the requirements of the program.

5. In our present circumstances, the budgetary aspect is a factor which must be taken into consideration to a greater degree.

6. In addition, clear locational and wayfinding signage for the visually, mobility, and developmentally impaired is deficient, particularly to emergency exiting routes.

7. The corporate financial function does not comprehensively challenge revenue plans and performance for the Department as a whole, thereby minimizing its input to revenue realization.

8. The acquisition, operation and disposal of vehicles can be significantly improved.

9. "Temporary pass" means a document which is designed to allow persons not entitled to a departmental identification card, or subject to the limitations contained therein, authorized access to departmental premises during silent hours for a limited period.

10. These various different agencies and offices that provide aid and assistance services to individual persons who participate in our program activities that we offer have reversed themselves back from the policy that they recently announced to return to the original policy that they followed earlier.

11. Decisions about the distribution of assistance funds should be made taking into consideration the following questions: Will the plan foster the conservation of existing stock through the preservation of housing deterioration? Will it foster the promotion of neighbourhood stability?

MODULE 4 — EXERCISE #1

12. The existing regulations are plagued with significant problems which render them inadequate to support the current regulatory program and incapable of meeting the challenge of expeditiously incorporating new regulatory obligations and commitments. The sheer complexity of the existing regulations results in an unnecessary waste of legislative drafters' precious time.

13. Timeliness of response, which usually depends on the proximity of rescue resources to incidents, is a critical factor in saving people in distress.

14. The present quarterly instalment requirements create problems in that at the time the first and second instalments, March 15 and June 15, are required to be made the tax liability for the prior year may not be known or assessed. Also, the option of estimating the liability for the current year requires a complicated calculation.

    To resolve these problems an additional option for the determination of quarterly instalments will make it simpler and more certain for quarterly remitters.

15. Where a cheque is tendered in payment, the name of the corporation must be entered on the face of the cheque.

16. As a non-resident who sojourned in Canada over 183 days in the calendar year, you are deemed to be a resident of Canada and not of a province. Therefore, you are not entitled to claim provincial tax credits.

17. We are recommending the employment of a three-month temporary public health dietician to provide staff relief and additional service in several high need mandatory program areas.

PLAIN LANGUAGE CLEAR AND SIMPLE

18. A thorough inspection of your forest home or summer cottage, and the surrounding property for obvious fire hazards is the first step in fire protection.

19. Respondents were concerned with management of the unit. Most of them judged the quality of supervisors' communication to be negative. They viewed the management of downsizing as ad hoc, without consultation and clear and accurate information. People had the impression of being cut adrift and left to their own devices.

EXERCISE

USING APPROPRIATE WORDS

SUGGESTED SOLUTIONS

1. Universal education and the demands of the changing economy mean that reading and writing are not the exclusive tools of educated people.

2. It is surprising how much Canadians enjoy pleasure reading particularly in light of the anxiety about poor reading levels in a society that is supposed to be so literate.

3. "Bias" means having an attitude or opinion about certain groups of people or things. A "stereotype" is a general opinion about a particular group which does not consider individual characteristics. When you apply the guidelines, review the material for words, images and situations that suggest a bias or a stereotype.

4. You must meet the requirements of the program before you apply.

5. In our present circumstances, cost must be considered more often.

6. As well, signs for the visually, mobility and developmentally impaired are not clear or understandable. The emergency exit signs are particularly poor.

7. The corporate financial department does not identify revenue plans and performance objectives for the department. As a result, the department cannot contribute to realizing a profit.

8. We can significantly improve the way we acquire, operate and dispose of vehicles.

9. A "temporary pass" is a document that enables you to temporarily access the department after hours. A temporary pass is issued to you if you are not entitled to a departmental identification card.

10. Various agencies assist people who participate in our program. These agencies are now following their original policy.

11. When you allocate assistance funds, please consider the following questions:

    - will the plan conserve existing stock by preventing housing from deteriorating?
    - will it promote neighbourhood stability?

12. The existing regulations are complex and have significant problems. The regulations cannot support the current regulatory program. Legislative drafters waste time trying to incorporate new regulatory obligations and commitments.

13. Quick response is critical in saving people in distress. The response time usually depends on how close rescue units are to where the incident occurs.

14. If you pay personal income tax in quarterly instalments, you have two options. Both options pose problems. If you base your instalments on an estimate of this year's tax payable, you have to go through complicated calculations. If you base your instalments on an estimate of this year's tax payable, you may have already paid your first instalments before you even know last year's tax payable.

    To make things simpler and more certain for you, Revenue Canada, Taxation, is providing you with a new option.

15. If you pay by cheque, be sure to write the name of the corporation on the front of it.

16. You lived in Canada as a non-resident for more than 183 days in the calendar year. We consider you to be a resident of Canada, but not a resident of a province. Therefore, you cannot claim provincial tax credits.

17. We recommend that the Department employ a public health dietitian for three months to provide staff relief and additional service in several mandatory programs that need assistance.

18. You can begin to protect your forest home or summer cottage from fire by inspecting your land and building(s) for obvious fire hazards.

19. Respondents were concerned with management of the unit. Most respondents considered that their supervisors communicated poorly. They thought that management dealt with reducing the size of the unit without planning ahead, without consulting staff and without providing clear and accurate information. They felt that they had been left to figure out for themselves what was going on and how to deal with it.

MODULE 5

WRITING CLEAR AND EFFECTIVE SENTENCES

Overview

This module focuses on the basic organizational unit of text – the sentence. Because sentences represent ideas, it is the sentence that builds the message for the reader. This module complements material in chapter 4 of *Plain Language: Clear and Simple*.

Objectives

By the end of this module, participants will see how writing clear and effective sentences will improve the quality of their writing and the readability of their message. They will understand the key techniques for building effective sentence structure. Participants will see how long, complicated sentences adversely affect their readers' understanding of their message. Participants will learn to get to the point quickly and not to overload a sentence with long preambles and modifying phrases or clauses. They will see the importance of using parallel constructions and including tabulation when writing about complex material.

Organization

This module is organized into the following sections:
1. The sentence
2. Write in the active voice
3. Use a positive tone

4. One idea to a sentence
5. Write clear, direct and short sentences
6. Keep the sentence core together
7. Eliminate surplus words
8. Use adverbs and adjectives sparingly
9. Avoid unnecessary preambles
10. Eliminate double negatives
11. Eliminate prepositional phrases
12. Place modifiers correctly
13. Put parallel ideas in parallel constructions
14. Use point form and lists appropriately

1. THE SENTENCE

The basic unit of writing is the sentence. Writers build ideas from sentence to sentence.

There are three parts in a sentence:

The department	*established*	*the grant program in 1989.*
Subject	Verb	Object

The simple, declarative sentence is the easiest way to process information. The reader can easily process who or what the actor or subject is, what the action or verb is, and the object of the action. Sentences that differ from the simple, declarative structure may cause readability problems.

2. WRITE IN THE ACTIVE VOICE

Sentences written in the active voice have an identifiable "actor." You know as soon as you read it who is doing what to whom.

> The manager wrote her report.

A sentence written in the passive voice puts the cart before the horse – the object or thing being acted upon is the subject.

> The report was written by the manager.

In some cases, the "actor" is not even part of the sentence.

> It was decided that the report should be written.

Who decided that the report should be written? Leaving out the subject makes the sentence harder to understand. It obscures who is responsible for the action. Replacing the missing subject and using the active voice clarifies the sentence and the reader's understanding.

Here are examples of the passive voice and suggested revisions:

EXAMPLE

Citizenship cannot be renounced merely by making a personal declaration to this effect.

Multiculturalism and Citizenship Canada
Dual Citizenship, 1992

Revised

You cannot renounce your citizenship merely by making a personal declaration.

EXAMPLE

The police look for facts that prove a crime occurred and that can be used as evidence in court. If there is sufficient evidence, and the alleged offender can be located, criminal charges can be laid.

Department of Justice Canada
What to do if a child tells you of sexual abuse, p. 5

Revised

The police look for facts that prove a crime occurred and that the crown attorney can use as evidence in court. If there is sufficient evidence, and the police can locate the alleged offender, they can lay criminal charges.

EXAMPLE

Although it is impossible to list every type of communication material issued by the federal government, the most common forms are included here.

Dept. of the Secretary of State of Canada
A Matter of Balance, 1988, p. 4

Revised

Although it is impossible to list every type of communication material issued by the federal government, we have included the most common forms here.

> **EXAMPLE**

> Two weeks after the initial mailing, a reminder card was sent to each member of the target sample. Three weeks after the reminder card a full package was sent to each individual who had not yet responded at that time. The survey period was completed four weeks after the last mailing.
>
> *Reading in Canada, 1991, Highlights, p. 3*
>
> **Revised**
>
> Two weeks after the initial mailing, we sent a reminder card to each member of the target sample. Three weeks after the reminder card, we sent a full package to each individual who had not yet responded at that time. The survey period ended four weeks after the last mailing.

You may want to use the passive voice sometimes. In the following example, the focus is on children who are sexually abused rather than the abuser. The passive voice is used to emphasize the victim.

> Many children who are victims of sexual abuse are told to keep what happened a secret. In most cases, they are bribed, intimidated or threatened. In some cases, the offender even uses physical force in efforts to keep the child from telling.
>
> *Department of Justice Canada*
> *What to do if a child tells you of sexual abuse*

Good Examples of Active Voice

EXAMPLE

Employers pay their workers every week, every two weeks or once a month. You can be paid in cash, by cheque or by direct deposit to your bank account. Your pay stub shows how much you earned. It also lists deductions for taxes, pension, unemployment insurance and any other items that are deducted from your pay.

Employment and Immigration Canada
Living in Canada, What You Should Know, 1993

The system first proved its worth only nine days after tests began. On Sept. 9, 1982, the Ottawa ground station picked up distress signals relayed by COSPAS 1 from a plane crash in northern British Columbia. The signals led searchers to the plane in a mountain valley 90 km off its planned route. Canadian Forces personnel rescued three injured survivors, in the world's first satellite-aided rescue operation.

Communications Canada
Space Facts

3. USE A POSITIVE TONE

Positive sentences are inviting and encourage people to read on. Negative sentences can seem bossy or hostile. They can cause your readers to mistrust your words and often discourage people from reading on. However, negative phrasing is appropriate for emphasizing danger, legal pitfalls or other warnings. You can also use negative phrasing to allay fears or dispel myths.

4. ONE IDEA TO A SENTENCE

Sentences containing more than one idea are called compound or complex sentences. The most common form of a compound sentence is two simple sentences connected with the conjunction "and." Compound or complex sentences can be readable. However, if you find more than one verb and one subject in the sentence, check to make sure you really want to connect the two ideas.

Here is an example of more than one idea in a sentence:

Some commercial sources such as second-hand bookstores, book exchanges or book banks, and book fairs featuring used books recycle previously purchased books and do not create new sales for the industry.

Communications Canada
Reading in Canada, 1991

Revised

Some commercial sources such as second-hand bookstores, book exchanges, book banks, and book fairs featuring used books recycle previously purchased books. They do not create new sales for the industry.

The revision creates two separate sentences.

Here is another example:

EXAMPLE

All travellers, including children, may be eligible for certain exemptions and as each traveller must also meet the entry requirements of several government agencies, it will be necessary for each person to complete a card.

Canada Customs Declaration Card

This complex sentence contains many ideas. It could be rewritten to separate the ideas.

Revised

All travellers, including children, must meet the entry requirements of several government agencies. Also, you may be eligible for certain exemptions. For these reasons, each person must complete a card.

The revision separates the original sentence into three ideas – the requirements of several agencies, the possibility of exemptions, and the reason for completing a card.

Here is another example:

EXAMPLE

All documents must be verified and applications must be found to be free of criminal and security prohibitions, so any clarification required in these areas may result in delays in processing.

Dealing with Canadian Citizenship Inquiries

Revised

There may be delays in processing citizenship applications. The delays can happen because all documents must be verified and applicants must not have any criminal and security prohibitions.

In the revised text, the first sentence is a simple sentence. The second sentence is a compound sentence. However, the compound sentence is easier to understand because it contains two ideas instead of the original three.

Writing that uses only simple sentences can be boring. Good writing uses a mixture of simple sentences and well-written compound sentences.

5. WRITE CLEAR, DIRECT AND SHORT SENTENCES

Research has shown that most people can retain between 15 and 25 words at one time. By the time your readers reach the end of a long sentence – or the middle of a really long one – they have forgotten the beginning.

Here are examples of long sentences and suggested revisions:

> The Government recognizes the Canada Council's vital role in assisting and nurturing the arts in Canada and will continue to review the financial requirements of the Council in light of both fiscal restraint and the desire of the artistic and academic research communities for increased financial resources and long-term stability.
>
> *Communications Canada*
> *Unique Among Nations, 1993*

Revised

We recognize the Canada Council's vital role in assisting and nurturing the arts in Canada. We also recognize that the artistic and academic research communities want increased funding and long-term stability. However, the need for fiscal restraint will affect our continuing review of the financial requirements of the Council.

TIP

YOU MAY BE ASKED...

Q. Isn't writing that is made up of only short sentences boring to read? It will sound too staccato.

A. Yes. The point here is to use shorter sentences and simple sentences more often than long sentences or complex sentences. Obviously, you will want to adjust your sentences so they flow easily. However, shorter sentences and simple sentences are more effective at communicating information.

EXAMPLE

And now with new Canadian standards for rating windows as well as incentive programs in certain provinces for consumers and builders using high-performance varieties, some manufacturers are working to bring their products up to the performance levels needed to qualify under the incentive programs.

Energy, Mines & Resources Canada
Partnership in Success, 1992

Revised

Some window manufacturers are working to improve their products because of new Canadian standards for rating windows and new incentive programs adopted by certain provinces. Consumers and builders will qualify for these programs if they use high-performance varieties.

Here is an example that uses short sentences to make its point:

EXAMPLE

The solution is simple. Don't take things that don't belong to you. Before you buy or borrow something from a friend, make sure that it's theirs to sell or lend. If your friends are involved in theft or break and enter, try to talk them out of it. If you can't, leave the scene, because you can also be charged.

Solicitor General Canada
Youth and the Law

An average sentence length of 15 to 25 words helps to improve the readability of your document. However, it doesn't guarantee readability. A well-organized, long sentence with tabulated points may be easier to follow than a poorly organized short sentence.

6. KEEP THE SENTENCE CORE TOGETHER

The sentence core is made up of the subject and the verb. A sentence is easy to read when these elements are close together.

"Left-branching" sentences are sentences with an extra phrase at the beginning. "Centre-embedded" sentences have an extra phrase in the middle. Sentences with these constructions are more difficult to read than "right-branching" sentences – those with an extra phrase at the end.

Dependent clauses often cause the branching problem. A dependent clause is a group of words that do not form a complete sentence. They often introduce related but separate ideas into a sentence – making the sentence more complex.

The most common form of dependent clause is the conditional clause at the beginning of a sentence. This construction results in a "left-branching" sentence as in the following example.

> **EXAMPLE**
>
> If the $20,000 past-service contribution had been paid after March 27, 1988, and not under a written agreement entered into before March 28, 1988, Morgan would calculate the amount he could deduct for 1991 under the limit that applies to past-service contribution while a contributor.
>
> *Revenue Canada*
> *Pensions – An RRSP Tax Guide, 1991*
>
> **Revised**
>
> Morgan would calculate the amount he could deduct in 1991 under the limit that applies to past-service contribution if the $20,000 past-service contribution:
> - had been paid after March 27, 1988, and
> - was not under a written agreement entered into before March 28, 1988.

The reader must first read and understand the condition, then read the core of the sentence. For long conditionals, like the above example, trying to keep all the information in short-term memory is too difficult.

Here are examples of left-branching and centre-embedded sentences and suggested revisions:

EXAMPLE

Our records indicate that on the date shown on the address label on the reverse side of this questionnaire, **you either completed this course or for some other reason, left the course early**.

Employment and Immigration

Revised

A date appears on the address label on the reverse side of this questionnaire. Our records indicate you either completed the course or left the course early on that date.

EXAMPLE

Bounded by the Coast Mountains to the west, the North British Columbia Mountains Region to the north, and the Rocky Mountains to the east, **the region comprises broad plateaus, valleys, highlands and mountains**.

Environment Canada
The State of Canada's Climate, 1992

Revised

The region comprises broad plateaus, valleys, highlands and mountains. It is bounded on the west by the Coast Mountains, on the north by the North British Columbia Mountains Region, and on the east by the Rocky Mountains.

> **EXAMPLE**
>
> **Suppliers** who employ 100 persons or more and who wish to, or are invited to, bid on contracts worth $200,000 or more with the federal government, **will first certify in writing their commitment to implement employment equity according to specific criteria.**
>
> *Employment and Immigration Canada*
> *Federal Contractors Program*
>
> **Revised**
>
> Suppliers will first certify in writing their commitment to implement employment equity according to specific criteria. This requirement applies to suppliers who employ 100 persons or more and who bid on contracts worth $200,000 or more with the federal government.

7. ELIMINATE SURPLUS WORDS

In any sentence, there are words that carry the real meaning of the sentence. There are also "glue" words that are necessary to hold the meaning words together, as well as "filler" words that may or may not amplify the meaning. As a plain language writer, your goal is to keep the meaning words and reduce the surplus words.

Here's a good way to sort the meaning from the filler words and reduce the surplus words in your writing.

Step 1: Circle the words that carry the essential meaning of the sentence.
Step 2: List the meaning words, then rearrange them in an order that directly conveys the meaning.
Step 3: Discard other unnecessary filler words as you rewrite the sentence. Add only the words you need to convey the meaning.

We began rewriting the following example by circling the meaning words.

EXAMPLE

(Aboriginal people and EIC) are (working together) (to establish) an (effective) (partnership) (to invest) in (developing and training) the (aboriginal labour force) for (participation) both in (unique) (aboriginal labour markets) and in the (broader Canadian labour market)

Government report

Here's an explanation for some of our choices.

- "Working together" and "partnership" suggest the same thing.
- "Effective" is redundant.
- In this context, the verbs "to establish" and "to invest" have no specific meaning. They just clutter up the sentence.
- "Unique" is an overused word which has lost its meaning in most writing.

After circling the meaning words, we listed them.

> Aboriginal people and EIC…working together…developing and training…aboriginal labour force…participation…aboriginal labour markets…broader Canadian labour market

Finally, we rewrote the sentence.

> Aboriginal people and EIC are working together to develop and train the aboriginal labour force for participation in aboriginal labour markets and the broader Canadian labour market.

8. USE ADVERBS AND ADJECTIVES SPARINGLY

Overwritten prose contains too many modifiers. You often hear someone say "it's the *honest* truth," or claim that a task is "*completely* finished." These words add length to a sentence without making the meaning clearer.

9. AVOID UNNECESSARY PREAMBLES

Sentences often begin with unnecessary preambles, phrases that weaken or hide the point they introduce. These preambles can usually be dropped without changing the meaning.

Here is a list of some unnecessary preambles:
- It is important to add that…
- It may be recalled that…
- In this regard it is of significance that…
- It is interesting to note that…

- Despite the fact that…
- Clear beyond dispute is the fact that…
- The point is…
- This is a situation in which…

"There are" and "it is" are often used unnecessarily. You should avoid beginning sentences with these preambles.

Here is an example of an unnecessary preamble and a suggested revision:

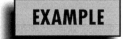

Unlike the *Citizenship Act* in effect in Canada up to 1977, the present Act allows a Canadian citizen to acquire a foreign nationality without automatically losing Canadian citizenship.

Multiculturalism and Citizenship Canada
Dual Citizenship, 1991

Revised

The *Citizenship Act* allows a Canadian citizen to acquire foreign nationality without automatically losing Canadian citizenship.

10. ELIMINATE DOUBLE NEGATIVES

By using double negatives you run the risk of overwhelming or confusing your readers. You can usually rewrite a sentence containing negating words in a more positive form, without one or more of the "not" words. This makes the sentence easier for your reader to understand the first time through. Using a positive approach helps to define responsibility more clearly, too.

11. ELIMINATE PREPOSITIONAL PHRASES

Usually prepositional phrases can easily be replaced with a single, simpler word. Here is a list of prepositional phrases and a list of simpler phrases to replace them.

Prepositional phrases	Replace with
at this (that) point in time	now (then)
as a consequence of	because of
by means of	by, under
by reason of	because of
by virtue of	by, under
for the purpose of	to
for the reason that	because
from the point of view of	from, for
in accordance with	by, under
in addition to	besides
inasmuch as	since
in association with	with
in case of	if
in connection with	with, about, concerning
in excess of	more than, over
in favour of	for
in order to	to
in relation to	about, concerning
insofar as	since
in the absence of	without
in the course of	during
in the event of/that	if
in the nature of	like
in the neighbourhood of	near
in the vicinity of	near
in view of	because of
on a daily basis	daily

Prepositional phrases (cont'd)	Replace with (cont'd)
on a regular basis	regularly
on the grounds of	because of
prior to	before
subsequent to	after
until such time as	until
with the exception of	except
with reference to	about, concerning
with regard to	about, concerning
with respect to	about, for, on

12. PLACE MODIFIERS CORRECTLY

The order of words within a sentence often affects the meaning of that sentence. Modifying words tend to do their work on whatever they are near. Therefore, be careful to put any modifying words as close as you can to the words you want them to modify.

Here is an example and a suggested revision:

EXAMPLE

My client has discussed your proposal to fill the drainage ditch with his partners.

Revised

My client has discussed with his partners your proposal to fill the drainage ditch.

13. PUT PARALLEL IDEAS IN PARALLEL CONSTRUCTIONS

Whenever a sentence includes a series of similar items, make sure that all items are in the same form. Describe each item using similarly constructed phrases. For example, use the same tense for all verbs that describe listed items.

EXAMPLE

Going on vacation…
- **Inform** a neighbour of your departure…
- **Have** your neighbour pick up newspapers…
- **Small** valuables should be stored…
- **Use** clock timers that activate lights…
- **Before** leaving, ensure all entries are secured…

Solicitor General Canada
Home Security

Revised

Going on vacation…
- **Inform** a neighbour of your departure…
- **Have** your neighbour pick up newspapers…
- **Store** small valuables…
- **Use** clock timers that activate lights…
- **Secure** all entries before leaving…

Parallel constructions often feature the use of conjunctions in pairs. Paired or correlative conjunctions are connectors that show similarity or difference. Common paired conjunctions include the following:

…as well as…
both…and…
either…or
neither…nor
not…but
not only…but also

Here is an example of the use of conjunctions and a suggested revision:

EXAMPLE

Plain language meets the audience's needs not only by using simpler writing and logical organization but also inviting design.

Revised

Plain language meets the audience's needs by using not only simpler writing and logical organization but also inviting design.

14. USE POINT FORM AND LISTS APPROPRIATELY

You can make parallel points clear and easy to remember by using tabulation or a dropped list. Each item in the list is preceded by a bullet or a number. Bullets or numbers draw the reader's attention and separate the items better than dashes.

Tabulation is an effective way to communicate complex information, procedures or instructions. Successful tabulation requires consistency in form and style. Variations in form or style only confuse the reader.

Here is an example of the good use of tabulation. In this example, the text before the bullets is called the lead-in. The text after the bullets is called the list.

Your representatives are your link to government. They can:

- represent your ideas when arguing for or against a proposed law;
- ask questions about the government on your behalf;
- present important issues;
- help you if you need services from government;
- help you find the right government or department to contact; and
- help you if you have a problem with any government.

Multiculturalism and Citizenship Canada
The Canadian Citizen, 1985

Here are some guidelines for tabulation:

1. The items in the list must form a logical group. Avoid making a list of (a) bread, (b) eggs and (c) the prime minister.

2. Each item should contain only one idea.

3. All items in the list should be in the same form. Avoid beginning some items with a noun and others with a verb. Avoid varying the tenses of the verbs you use in a list.

4. Each item should work separately with the lead-in to form a complete sentence. Concluding material must fit in too if the sentence continues after the last item on the list.

5. Put anything common to all items in the lead-in.

6. The list should be indented to set it apart from the lead-in and any concluding material. Return to the left margin for any statement following the list.

7. Use bullets to identify each item in the list. Use numbers instead of bullets only when you are describing step-by-step procedures. Avoid using both numbers and bullets in a list.

8. If bullets are being used, all items in the list should begin with a lower case letter.

9. When items contain commas or are lengthy, use semicolons at the end of each item; otherwise use commas or no punctuation. Put a period after the last item if it is the end of the sentence.

10. If the list consists of alternatives, put "or" after the second last item. If the list is inclusive, put "and" after the second last item.

EXERCISE

WRITING CLEAR AND EFFECTIVE SENTENCES

Have participants review one or more of the following paragraphs. For each paragraph, have them identify the "problem" or "issue" from the point of view of clear and effective sentences. Then, have participants rewrite the sentences to improve the paragraph's clarity. Participants can work individually, and then discuss their results in small groups.

1. Illiterate adults are not able to read most work written for adults. Most illiterate adults are, however, adult thinkers. Nevertheless, they are often unable to carry out democratic tasks like voting. They are, however, fully capable of making decisions required for such tasks.

2. You use this package to report the income to both the federal government and the province of Ontario. The taxes you pay to the federal government and the province are calculated differently. The Ontario tax rate is a percentage of the basic federal tax. The form you use to claim these credits is included with the other schedules in this package.

3. Collaboration takes many forms. Companies develop new services and products in consultation with suppliers and clients. They enter strategic alliances with foreign companies to build a market share. They launch adopt-a-school programs so that they can help train a new generation of Canadians for a knowledge-intensive global marketplace. But perhaps nowhere is the impact of collaboration felt more strongly than in science and technology. Innovation, through science and technology, is vital to businesses of all sizes in all

PLAIN LANGUAGE **CLEAR** AND **SIMPLE**

sectors of the economy. Innovation intensifies productivity. It helps companies build niche markets in higher value-added production. It gives them the flexibility to respond to new market opportunities when they emerge.

4. The engineers have recommended sealing the panel cracks and monitoring the situation, which they believe does not constitute a problem with respect to the structural integrity of the panels.

5. Both buildings were found to have features that impede accessibility for the handicapped, whether employees or clients of the government, and breached not only the National Building Code (NBC) in effect at the time of construction but also the subsequent Treasury Board directives for improving accessibility in existing government buildings, specifically with respect to wheelchair ramps, washrooms, door hardware, wayfinding and car parking.

6. Shortly before Bill C-69 was introduced in Parliament, the province of British Columbia asked the British Columbia Court of Appeal whether the Government of Canada had any authority to limit its obligations under the Canada Assistance Plan, and whether the terms of the Agreement pursuant to the Plan between the governments of Canada and British Columbia gave rise to a legitimate expectation that the Government of Canada would not seek to limit its obligations under that Agreement without the consent of British Columbia.

7. The Department promotes activities that help achieve and maintain environmental standards. These include identifying sources and causes of pollution; advising on ways to prevent pollution and restore the environment; regulating the introduction, transportation, use and disposal of toxic substances; and enforcing environmental laws and regulations.

8. It is hoped that this directory will provide a valuable resource for all of Canada's business people.

9. The guidelines apply to all internal and external federal government communications, including written, visual (slides, films, posters, publication covers, graphics, advertising) and oral (speeches, voice-overs, dialogues) material produced by the federal government or contracted for or purchased from the public sector.

10. At the same time, the economic approach pursued by this study to highlight the importance of volunteer work does not imply that organized volunteer work should be regarded as a commercial economic activity, as this term is normally understood.

EXERCISE #1 – SUGGESTED SOLUTIONS   MODULE 5

EXERCISE

WRITING CLEAR AND EFFECTIVE SENTENCES

SUGGESTED SOLUTIONS

1. **Issues:**
   - use a positive tone, and
   - put parallel ideas in parallel construction.

   Solution:
   Illiterate adults may have difficulty reading work written for adults. They may also have difficulty with democratic tasks like voting. However, illiterate adults are adult thinkers and they are capable of making the decisions required for these tasks.

2. **Issues:**
   - place modifiers correctly,
   - use a positive tone,
   - avoid chains of nouns, and
   - split material into two paragraphs.

   Solution:
   Companies collaborate in many ways. They:
   - develop new products and services with their suppliers and clients,
   - develop relationships with foreign companies to build market share, and
   - launch adopt-a-school programs to help train Canadian children.

PLAIN LANGUAGE **CLEAR** AND **SIMPLE**

Collaboration is more evident, though, in science and technology. It helps companies introduce new products and services which:
- is vital for all businesses,
- increases productivity,
- helps companies build niche markets, and
- enables companies to respond to new market opportunities.

3. **Issues:**
   - write in the active voice,
   - limit one idea to a sentence, and
   - eliminate prepositional phrases.

   Solution:
   The engineers recommend sealing the panel cracks and monitoring the situation. They believe this recommendation will improve the structural quality of the panels.

4. **Issues:**
   - write in the active voice,
   - limit one idea to a sentence,
   - use tabulation,
   - eliminate surplus words,
   - use verbs rather than nouns, and
   - eliminate prepositional phrases.

EXERCISE #1 – SUGGESTED SOLUTIONS   MODULE 5

Solution:

We found features in both buildings that make accessing the buildings difficult for persons with disabilities. We also found that the buildings were not constructed according to the National Building Code (NBC). The buildings also do not conform to the Treasury Board's instructions for improving access to government buildings. These instructions apply to:

- wheelchair ramps,
- washrooms,
- door hardware,
- signs, and
- car parking.

5. **Issues:**
    - write clear, direct and short sentences,
    - avoid unnecessary preambles,
    - eliminate surplus words, and
    - limit one idea to a sentence.

    Solution:

    The province of British Columbia asked the British Columbia Court of Appeal whether the Government of Canada had to fulfil all of its obligations under the Canada Assistance Plan. They also asked whether the terms of their agreement for the Canada Assistance Plan stated that the government of Canada could limit its obligations without first asking British Columbia.

6. **Issues:**
   - use tabulation, and
   - use verbs rather than nouns.

   Solution:
   The Department promotes activities that help achieve and maintain environmental standards. These include:
   - identifying sources and causes of pollution;
   - recommending ways to prevent pollution and restore the environment;
   - regulating the ways that toxic substances are introduced transported, used and disposed of; and
   - enforcing environmental laws and regulations.

7. **Issue:**
   - write in the active voice.

   Solution:
   We hope that this directory will be a valuable resource for all Canadian business people.

8. **Issues:**
   - limit one idea to a sentence, and
   - write in the active voice.

   Solution:
   There may be delays in processing your application. The delays can happen because all documents must be verified and applicants must not have any criminal or security prohibitions.

EXERCISE #1 – SUGGESTED SOLUTIONS

MODULE 5

9. **Issues:**
   - use tabulation, and
   - eliminate surplus words.

   Solution:
   The guidelines apply to all internal and external communications material produced by the federal government or contracted for or purchased from the private sector. Communications material includes:
   - written material;
   - visual material (slides, films, posters, publication covers, graphics, advertising); and
   - oral material (speeches, voice-overs, dialogues).

10. **Issues:**
    - keep the sentence core together, and
    - avoid chains of nouns.

    Solution:
    The study highlights the importance of volunteer work. The financial approach included in the study does not imply that organized volunteer work should be seen as a sales activity.

PLAIN LANGUAGE **CLEAR** AND **SIMPLE**

MODULE 6

WRITING CLEAR AND EFFECTIVE PARAGRAPHS

Overview

This module focuses on writing effective paragraphs. Participants can focus on paragraphs only after they have written their ideas into sentences. The purpose of the paragraph is to link all the ideas in a topic. This module complements material in chapter 4 of *Plain Language: Clear and Simple*.

Objectives

By the end of this module, participants will see how writing clear and effective paragraphs will improve the structure and organization of a document and the readability of their message. They will understand how well-written paragraphs break up the text into manageable chunks of information resulting in easier reading and better comprehension. Participants will learn to analyze the function of each paragraph. They will see how the sentences within each paragraph, and the paragraphs of a document, should progress logically.

Organization

This module is organized into three sections:
1. The purpose of a paragraph
2. The structure of a paragraph
3. The use of transitions

1. THE PURPOSE OF A PARAGRAPH

The purpose of a paragraph is to develop a single topic. A good length for a paragraph is three to five sentences. Short paragraphs don't guarantee readability, but they do help to break up information into manageable chunks.

2. THE STRUCTURE OF A PARAGRAPH

A good paragraph should have a beginning, a middle and an end. It usually begins with a general statement, the topic sentence. The sentences which follow express specific ideas related to that topic. Every sentence in a paragraph should be linked to the sentence which precedes it, or to the topic sentence itself.

You can relate each sentence to the paragraph topic by chaining ideas or by linking them directly to the topic sentence.

2.1 Chaining ideas

Near the beginning of each sentence, refer to a key word from the previous sentence, by repeating it or by using a pronoun or a synonym. Each sentence then refers to the topic sentence indirectly through the chain of topics. Here is an example where ideas are chained:

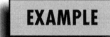

Very often we, in government and administration, have to set up **new categories**. Only certain people in a **category** can receive assistance. We don't have a **special word for this category**; so what we do is decide that we will take an everyday word and give it **special meaning**. We salve our conscience by saying. "Oh, I've put it in the **definitions section** so people ought to refer to it there." We ignore the fact that many **readers** don't know about **definitions sections** and are not used to using them. We also ignore the fact that we place a great psychological strain on **readers**; we define a word in the beginning of the text and then expect them to remember its **special use** through 170-odd pages.

Robert Eagleson, 1988

2.2 Linking each sentence to the main topic

At or near the beginning of each sentence, refer to the topic by repeating the topic itself, or by using a pronoun or a synonym. Each sentence in the paragraph will then refer directly to the topic sentence. Here is an example:

Think of the **long sentence**. How many of us hate the **long sentence**? How many of us decry **it**, and yet how many of us produce **it** when we're writing? We hate others to impose the **long sentence** on us, but we're happy to produce **it** ourselves.

Robert Eagleson, 1988

There are many ways to organize a paragraph. You can group ideas within the paragraph by using one of the following orders:
- cause, then effect;
- chronology;
- facts, then opinion;
- general, then particular situation;
- precedent, then application:
- proposal, then response;
- question, then answer;
- requirement, then justification; and
- rule, then exceptions.

3. THE USE OF TRANSITIONS

A transition is a word, phrase, sentence or paragraph that shows the relationship between two or more parts of your writing. They help your writing move smoothly from idea to idea, sentence to sentence, section to section. Transitions help the reader to understand the logical or chronological relationships that are familiar to you.

Simple chronological transitions indicate the order of events. Chronological transitions can also be used to help readers anticipate the sequence of points or ideas. Logical transitions can show cause, contrast, similarity or conclusion.

If you find that you have one or two favourite transition words, particularly "however," you may be trying to compensate for poorly organized text. Use transition words when you need them, but avoid overusing them.

List of Transition Words

Similarity
again
also
and
as a matter of fact
as well
besides
for example
for instance
furthermore
in addition
in other words
in particular
indeed
moreover
namely
similarly
specifically
that is

Contrast
although
but
conversely
despite this
however
instead
nevertheless
on the contrary
still
yet

Conclusion
in conclusion
in short
in summary
on the whole
to summarize
finally
first, next, last
immediately
later
meanwhile
next
presently
previously
since
soon
subsequently
then
while

Cause
as a result
accordingly
because
consequently
for
hence
if… then
since
so
thus

Sequence
afterwards
at last
at length
at the same time
eventually

EXERCISE

WRITING CLEAR AND EFFECTIVE PARAGRAPHS

Have participants work with one or more of the following paragraphs. For each paragraph, have them identify the "problem" or "issue" from the point of view of clear and effective paragraphs. Then, have participants rewrite the paragraph. Participants can work individually, and then discuss their results in small groups.

1. Exploring the Community

   The advantages of this is that its demands are based on day-to-day experience, that its scope is flexible, and that it allows the teacher to gain a full measure of insight into parents' lives. The first task is to explain to students that the community is its people and then to have them list family members and to go home and gather stories and objects which their parents consider to be of special significance. The objects should be displayed and the stories shared. Once this has been done parents should be invited to come and elaborate or to tell new stories themselves. The project can end at this point with family portraits, family trees, family histories, travel journals, biographies, etc. It can, however, be expanded to take in the entire neighbourhood. In this case, it may culminate in the preparation of street maps, the drawing up of bar graphs (on the relationship between one- and two-storey houses in a five-block section, for instance), the making of models of places of interest, the recording of interviews with local businessmen, the consideration of local concerns, the production of neighbourhood directories or tourist guides. Parents can take part in all these ventures – helping to make contacts for research purposes, accompanying groups or individuals on measuring or sketching expeditions, acting as guides for field trips to churches, synagogues, stores, and restaurants, finding materials, giving advice. They can be invited to view work in progress or at the time it is complete.

2. The new user fee policy indicates that full costs for the provision of facilities and services to external users should be known and recovered unless there are valid reasons to do otherwise. Compromising the objective of the program or other government goals, or an unacceptably adverse impact on the financial position of users, are two such reasons. The policy also indicates that a fee can exceed costs, such as in the case of issuance of limited rights and privileges, but reminds the departments to have the necessary authority. However, departments do not always have a cost recovery policy and related procedures to help determine where program objectives could be enhanced or might be impaired, or to determine where costs and other measures would be necessary to establish appropriate fees.

3. A variety of activities can be used to bring compliance with the law. Compliance promotion includes educating companies and the public on the requirements of the law on ways to avoid pollution. It also includes assistance in the form of technology and of tax or other economic incentives. Enforcement includes activities designed to detect violations to require correction or, as appropriate, to collect evidence and prosecute violators. Enforcement measures can range from warnings and directives to fines and imprisonment.

4. The express lanes project was tried at a tunnel crossing into Ontario from 27 August to 14 December 1990. Like the special lanes project, travellers qualified only if they had no goods to declare. Unlike the other project, users had to first apply for an identification symbol for their vehicle and an individual permit. Customs, with assistance from Immigration officials, performed background checks and approved the application only if the applicant had no criminal record or record of other violation of Customs and Immigration laws. Approved users placed their symbol in the front windshield and proceeded slowly through dedicated express lanes, showing their permit. Customs inspectors checked for the symbol and the permit and did not have to stop the vehicle for questioning.

5. Neither project has been successful because of the low utilization rates. Although 11 percent of travellers qualified for the special lanes at two of the bridges, only 0.5 percent used them. In fact, the project at these two sites was discontinued after five weeks, seven weeks ahead of schedule. Regular lanes were processing about 125 vehicles an hour; the special lane was only processing, on average, 3 vehicles an hour. At the third site about 40 vehicles an hour were processed in the special lanes, compared with 100 to 140 vehicles in regular lanes, and this project was completed as scheduled. Utilization of the express lanes at the tunnel crossing averaged 65 vehicles an hour and was up to 105 vehicles from 5 p.m. to 6 p.m. on weeknights. However, the regular lanes were processing 210 vehicles an hour in the same time period. As no stopping was required in the express lanes, their use was well below capacity.

EXERCISE

WRITING CLEAR AND EFFECTIVE PARAGRAPHS

SUGGESTED SOLUTIONS

1. **Issues:**
   - use topic sentence,
   - limit one topic to a paragraph,
   - use transition words properly,
   - limit one idea to a sentence,
   - use tabulation,
   - use words your reader will understand,
   - write clear, direct and short sentences, and
   - write in the active voice.

   Solution:
   The Exploring the Community project is working well in our school. The advantages of Exploring the Community are that:
   - the demands of the project are based on day-to-day experiences,
   - the scope of the project is flexible, and
   - teachers gain an insight into parents' lives.

   The teachers have developed an excellent procedure for the project. They start by talking to the students about their community. It is important that the students understand that the community is its people.

The next step is to have the students list all of the members of their family. The students can then go home and gather stories and objects that have special significance to the community.

The third step is to share the stories and objects. This should be done first with the students. Then, the parents can be invited to elaborate on the stories or tell some of their own.

The project can end at this point with family portraits, family histories, travel journals, biographies, etc. It can, however, be expanded to include the entire neighbourhood. In this case, the project might also include:
- preparing street maps;
- drawing bar graphs (showing the relationship between one- and two-storey houses in a five-block section, for example);
- making models of interesting places;
- recording interviews with local business people; and
- producing neighbourhood directories or tourist guides.

Parents can take part in all of these additional steps. They can:
- help to make contacts for research purposes;
- accompany students on, measure, or sketch expeditions;
- act as guides for field trips to churches, synagogues, stores and restaurants;
- find material; and
- give advice.

2. **Issues:**
   - limit one topic to a paragraph,
   - link sentences in the paragraph,
   - eliminate surplus words,
   - avoid chains of nouns,
   - limit one idea to a sentence,
   - use verbs rather than nouns,
   - use tabulation, and
   - eliminate prepositional phrases.

Solution:

The new policy for user fees indicates that we should identify and recover full costs when we provide facilities and services to external users. However, there are two reasons why we would not recover the full cost. They are:
   1. The objective of the program or other government goals would be compromised.
   2. The external users could not afford to pay the full costs.

The policy also indicates that the fee we charge the external user can exceed the full costs. This is the case, for example, when we issue limited rights and privileges. We must get proper authority to exceed costs for the fee.

Some departments do not have a policy or procedures for cost recovery. The policy and procedures help determine:
   - where program objectives could be enhanced,
   - where program objectives might be impaired, and
   - what costs and other measures would have to be necessary to establish appropriate fees.

3. **Issues:**
   - use topic sentence,
   - limit one topic to a paragraph, and
   - use tabulation.

   Solution:
   We use a variety of activities to ensure that companies and the public comply with pollution laws. They include educating companies and the public about ways to avoid pollution. As well, we provide technology and tax or other economic incentives.

   We enforce the laws by designing activities that detect violators and ensure that they correct the situation. If necessary, we also collect evidence and prosecute violators.

   People who violate the pollution laws are:
   - given a warning,
   - ordered to stop polluting,
   - given a fine, or
   - sent to prison.

4. **Issues:**
   - link sentences in the paragraph,
   - limit one topic to a paragraph,
   - avoid unnecessary preambles,
   - write in the active voice,
   - keep the sentence core together, and
   - limit one idea to a sentence.

   Solution:
   We tried the express lanes project at a tunnel crossing into Ontario. The project lasted from August 27 to December 14, 1990.

   First, travellers had to qualify for the project. To qualify, travellers were not allowed to declare any goods.

   After qualifying, travellers had to apply for an identification symbol for their vehicle with an individual permit. Customs performed background checks on each traveller with assistance from Immigration officials. Applications were approved only if the traveller had no criminal record or record of violating a Customs and Immigration law.

   Once approved, travellers could use the express lanes. To use them, travellers:
   - placed their identification symbol in the front windshield of their car,
   - proceeded slowly through the express lanes, and
   - showed their permit to the Customs Inspectors.

   Travellers passed more quickly through the tunnel into Ontario with the designated express lanes. Customs Inspectors checked for the symbol and the permit and didn't have to stop the travellers for questioning.

5. **Issues:**
   - limit one topic to a paragraph,
   - use transition words properly,
   - limit one idea to a sentence, and
   - use verbs rather than nouns.

   Solution:
   We tried two different projects at border crossings to help travellers pass more quickly into Ontario. The projects were not successful because travellers were not using the lanes.

   The special lanes project was set up at three sites. At two of the sites, 11% of travellers qualified for the lanes, but only .5% actually used them. On average, the special lanes only processed three vehicles an hour. The regular lanes processed about 125 vehicles an hour. The project at these two sites was discontinued after five weeks, which was seven weeks ahead of schedule. At the third site, the special lanes processed 40 vehicles an hour. The regular lanes processed up to 140 vehicles an hour. The project was completed on time at the third site.

   The express lanes project was set up at a tunnel crossing. The express lanes processed about 65 vehicles an hour. Up to 105 vehicles were processed in the express lanes between 5 p.m. and 6 p.m. on weeknights. However, the regular lanes processed 210 vehicles an hour in the same period. Since travellers were not required to stop in the express lanes, they were not being used as much as they could have been.

MODULE 7

PRESENTING YOUR MESSAGE EFFECTIVELY

Overview

This module describes how to effectively present your message. The way you present information on the page is just as important as the words and sentences you use. A well-written document is harder to read if it is poorly laid out. A good format highlights important information, links related sections and separates others. How your document looks can make the difference between your message being understood or lost. This module complements material in chapter 6 of *Plain Language: Clear and Simple*.

Objectives

By the end of this module, participants will understand that clear and effective design and presentation is an important part of a clear message. They will see that a design that fits the form and function of a document can make the document easier to read and that inappropriate design can affect the readability of even a well-written document. Participants will learn how to develop appropriate text and page layout and how to evaluate effective use of colour, graphics and illustrations.

Organization

This module is organized into the following sections:
1. Text and readability
   - type style and size
   - spacing
2. Page format
   - justification
3. Headings and subheadings
4. Highlighting
5. Table of contents
6. Visual effectiveness
   - colour of ink and paper
   - graphics and illustrations

1. TEXT AND READABILITY

1.1 Type style and size

Choose a solid, plain type style which is easy to read. Avoid combining many different type styles on the same page because it gives a document a very busy, confusing appearance. Different type styles should be used consistently, but only occasionally, for emphasis or to set some information apart.

Make sure the type size is big enough for your readers. People will often skip over text which is too small. Small type makes a document look crammed and uninviting. A 12-point type size is a good average size to use. Be sure to consider that seniors or people with visual impairments prefer a larger type size.

Avoid using capital letters to emphasize large blocks of text. In ALL CAPS, all word shapes are rectangular and less familiar to the reader. In upper and lower case, words have distinct shapes that are more easily recognized. Text in ALL CAPS is harder to read, especially for more than a few words, as this example shows:

TEXT SET IN ALL-CAPITALS IS HARDER TO READ
THAN TEXT SET IN UPPER AND LOWER CASE.
RESEARCHERS HAVE FOUND THAT PEOPLE READ
CONTINUOUS CAPITAL LETTERS AT A SLOWER
RATE THAN SMALL LETTERS.

ALL CAPS can be useful to draw attention to headings or a brief statement, such as:

PLEASE PRINT

Use serif type styles for body text – the main text of your document. Serif type styles make text easier to read. They have small embellishments or "hooks" on the letters that help the eye move along the line. These serifs also give readers extra clues about letters and words by defining their shapes more clearly. Palatino, Times Roman, CG Times and Bookman are all examples common serif type styles.

Use a contrasting sans serif type style for headings and subheadings. The type size of headings should be noticeably larger than the text or in boldface for further contrast. Helvetica and Univers are examples of common sans serif type styles.

1.2 Spacing

Long paragraphs without lists or summaries are difficult to read. Keep your paragraphs short, generally no more than four or five sentences. Leave space between paragraphs.

Divide your document into sections of related information.

Avoid printing on every inch of space on your page. For example, if you are using a column format, use only two columns for your text on a three-column page. Part of the extra white space can be used to draw attention to important information in boxes or boldface type.

Be generous with margin space.

2. PAGE FORMAT

2.1 Justification

Use unjustified or ragged right hand margins instead of using right or full justification. When text is printed with a justified right margin, the words on longer lines are spaced closer together, while the words on shorter lines are spread further apart, to even out the lines. Constantly adjusting to these changes in spacing is tiring to the eyes.

Right justification can produce a lot of hyphenated words, which present another reading challenge.

Compare these texts:

RIGHT JUSTIFICATION	RAGGED RIGHT MARGIN
Technology, like international competition and the emergence of an integrated world economy, is changing the way Canadians work. Computers are familiar pieces of equipment in offices and factories, and Canadians working on the shop floor and in the boardroom are having to learn new tasks. The new workplace skills require more education, more training, better communication and higher levels of literacy. Skilled minds are taking over from the skilled hands of yesteryear.	Technology, like international competition and the emergence of an integrated world economy, is changing the way Canadians work. Computers are familiar pieces of equipment in offices and factories, and Canadians working on the shop floor and in the boardroom are having to learn new tasks. The new workplace skills require more education, more training, better communication and higher levels of literacy. Skilled minds are taking over from the skilled hands of yesteryear.

3. HEADINGS AND SUBHEADINGS

If you use clear headings and subheadings, readers can find specific information in your document faster and more easily. Some sample headings that can capture your reader's attention are:
- How can I get help right away?
- What is a preliminary inquiry?
- What you can do
- Where to find answers and information on drugs

4. HIGHLIGHTING

Use boxes to separate key information from the rest of your text. Information in a box stands out more on the page.

Highlight headings, words or phrases with boldface type, but be careful not to overuse it. If only a few words or phrases are highlighted, the reader will notice them even when just glancing at the page.

Other types of highlighting are:
- Bullets. Use them for point form lists and summaries. They can be stylized as arrows or miniature graphics.
- Italic print. Use it to emphasize a phrase or word, as in, "I told him he could do the project, but on *his* time!" Italics are also used for phrases in other languages or for titles of publications. Avoid overusing italic print because it is difficult to read in large amounts.

- Underlining. Use it under titles or to add emphasis.
- Colour. Use it to add interest to the page, if your budget permits. Shaded areas can also be used to set text apart.

5. TABLE OF CONTENTS

Add a table of contents at the beginning of long documents. It tells readers about the organization of your document and makes it easy to find information. Although this is useful to all readers, it is especially important for people with low reading skills, who cannot skim through your document quickly and easily.

6. VISUAL EFFECTIVENESS

6.1 Colour of ink and paper

- Use a dark ink, such as navy blue or black, on light paper (white or cream). However, seniors or people with visual impairments find grey ink difficult to read.
- Avoid colour combinations with low contrast, such as blue with green, or pink or yellow on white.
- Avoid large passages of light print on black background.

6.2 Graphics and illustrations

You can add interest to your document with illustrations, photographs, diagrams, lines and symbols. However, use graphics cautiously. Make sure that they mean the same thing to your reader as they do to you. Ask people who would be using your document to look over your choice of graphics and illustrations. Are the symbols easily recognizable? Do the lines help guide the reader?

Tables, charts and graphs can be useful for anyone familiar with them. However, these visual aids are generally more difficult to use and you cannot assume that people understand them. So make sure you are using graphics and illustrations that are appropriate for your reading audience.

The right kind of visual aids can help your reader understand your message and remember what you have written. Place all graphics and illustrations as close as possible to the text they refer to.

EXERCISE

PRESENTING YOUR MESSAGE EFFECTIVELY

Use documents from your participants' program area. Have participants look at the material and identify examples of effective and ineffective presentation of information.

Have the group discuss what they have identified.

Depending on the document being evaluated, there will be a number of different design issues. Here are some issues that you may want to focus the discussion around:

- minimum type size of 10 or 12 point,
- serif type style,
- justified left and ragged right text,
- short paragraphs with plenty of white space,
- table of contents in larger documents,
- clear headings and subheadings,
- appropriate highlighting,
- dark ink on light paper, and
- appropriate and understandable graphics and illustrations.

MODULE 8

TESTING AND REVISING THE DOCUMENT FOR USABILITY AND READABILITY

Overview

This module discusses ways to get feedback on documents before they are sent out to readers. Normally, this involves testing the documents. The module discusses both formal methods that can be used to field test documents for comprehension and usability, as well as informal methods of getting feedback. The module also discusses what to do with the test results. This module complements material in chapter 7 of *Plain Language: Clear and Simple*.

Objectives

By the end of this module, participants will understand that testing the success of a document is a crucial part of the plain language process. They will learn the importance of knowing that their readers will easily read and understand their message. Participants will learn about testing methods and when to use various methods.

Organization

This module is organized into the following sections:
1. What is document testing?
2. Why test a document?
3. When should a document be tested?
4. How to test a document for usability and readability
5. What to do with the test results

1. WHAT IS DOCUMENT TESTING?

An important part of the plain language process is testing your document with the intended audience. After you think that you have designed an appropriate message, the next step is to test that message to make sure it works. Testing helps ensure that the document meets both the needs of the audience and your needs.

Sometimes document testing is called usability testing or readability testing. This is because when you test a document you want to find out if the intended audience can understand and use the information.

2. WHY TEST A DOCUMENT?

Testing helps ensure that your document meets the needs of your readers before you print and distribute it. You and your colleagues invest a lot of time and energy in order to communicate effectively through a document or form. Too often, we only find out about miscommunication when it is too late – when the problems occur after we have distributed a document. Testing helps to ensure that your investment in communication is well spent and gives you the knowledge that your document is effective.

TIP

YOU MAY BE TOLD...

We don't have time to test.

A. Testing is one of the most ignored areas of plain language. You may not have time to test. However, you should make that decision knowing that the document may not communicate effectively and you may end up spending more money trying to "fix" the communication after. You will get feedback. The issue is whether you want the feedback when you can still do something about it or after the brochure or document is already in the field.

3. WHEN SHOULD A DOCUMENT BE TESTED?

Testing gets better results when the documents are in final form. Test documents should resemble as much as possible the product that you plan to give your audience. This means using the colour and graphics in your test document that you plan to use in your final document. It also means printing your document with the same text layout and paper size that you will use for the final product.

Testing can also be a very effective way to get feedback on documents that are currently in use before revising them. A thorough knowledge of problems with current documents helps you avoid making the same mistakes as the previous writers.

4. HOW TO TEST A DOCUMENT FOR USABILITY AND READABILITY

There are many methods of testing a document or form. These range from the formal to the very informal.

4.1 Formal methods

This section outlines the process for testing public-use forms and documents. The formal method involves the following steps.

4.1.1 Identify what is most important.

Formal testing can give you a great deal of information. The variables that you identify depend on the type and purpose of the document. Depending on the document, you may want to focus the test on:
- what are the general impressions of the document,
- what image of the service is presented by the document,
- how easily can users find information,
- how well users understand the information, and
- how well readers can use the information (for example, can users fill out an application based on its instructions or access a government service based on a step-by-step procedure).

Test participants can be asked to consider such questions as:
- What is your first impression of the document?
- What do you like or dislike about the document?
- What message do you get from the document?
- How would you use the document?
- How does the document compare with other, similar documents?
- What experiences have you had with related programs and services?
- Can you do what the document tells you to do? How easy or difficult is it to understand? To follow instructions? To complete a form?

Testing is often used to assess people's information needs and knowledge of services. For example, participants may be asked to consider where they would go to get the information they need. This gives the tester some idea of where and how a document could be distributed. Participants might be asked to describe experiences they have had with written information about specific programs and services.

4.1.2 Identify test group(s).

You should test the document or form with members of the intended audience. Whether you test it with one group or many groups depends on how many different "audiences" you have for the document. Usually there are many audience segments, each with different characteristics. The number of segments helps you decide how many groups to test.

For example, if 50% of your audience is urban and 50% is rural, you should set up the groups so that 50% are urban and 50% are rural. This is called stratifying the groups. If a segment of the audience has special needs (for example, low reading skills) then you may want to sample more among this audience to make sure that their needs are met.

When testing documents or forms, you do not need a large number of people in the groups. Data analysis seldom includes statistical tests for differences, so scientific sampling is seldom used for testing plain language documents. When testing a widely distributed form, for example, a group of about 40–50 people is sufficient.

4.1.3 Choose an appropriate way to test.

In this section, we give a brief outline of four methods that can be used. In some situations, such as those having both forms and information brochures, you may want to use more than one method. Each of the following methods has its strengths and weaknesses.

Remember, the purpose of testing is to see how the document or form is used. This means testing the document as it will really look by printing a small number of the final form or document. It also means using a method or setting that re-creates (as closely as possible) how the document will be used. For example, an information brochure is often meant to be scanned or picked up on impulse from a rack. In this case, a focus group method would be appropriate. Forms, on the other hand, require more in-depth analysis of how the individual completes the form. Individual testing would be appropriate in this case.

1. **Focus Group Testing.** Focus group testing is a process of getting 8 to 10 people from the audience together. The moderator of the group leads the discussion of the document. This discussion focuses the group on such things as:
   - what are the first impressions,
   - what is the impact of the document,
   - how the document can be used, and
   - how easy is it to locate information.

   This type of testing is very effective for general information brochures or overviews of programs and services. It is not a very useful method when testing for comprehension or for testing forms.

2. **Scenario Testing.** This method tests the document or form with individuals, one at a time. It involves setting up a "scenario" that the target audience might use. Using this scenario, each individual is asked to fill out the form or read the document. The participant is observed during this process so that any problem areas on the form or in the document can be corrected. In very sophisticated testing, video cameras record the event for later analysis. Then, a series of questions is asked of the respondent about the exercise. These questions can cover general variables such as what the respondent thought about the form or document, or specific questions about whether the respondent understood specific words, directions and other parts of the form.

For example, in a recent project to create a plain language insurance policy and forms, the current documents were evaluated with scenario testing. Participants were given a fictitious name and details about an accident in which they had been involved. Some of the participants were asked to find and read sections of the policy that covered their situation. Their comprehension was tested with a series of questions. The remaining participants were asked to complete insurance applications and forms based on the "scenario." The ability of the participants to find and understand information in the policy or correctly complete the applications and forms was noted by the facilitators. Errors made and questions asked were also noted.

3. **Field Surveys.** Where focus group testing or scenario testing would not work, it is often useful to test the document through individual interviews or questionnaires. For example, it is often difficult to recruit focus groups among professionals. In this case, the document or form may be sent to a sample of individuals. Then a time to interview them is set up. The interviewer can ask questions about the document such as the impact the document had, whether it was easy to read, or whether there were parts of the document that were not clear.

4. **Site Testing.** Site testing is often called "beta" testing. This is because the test is considered a test of the "second" version of the document. The first version is the draft that you have been working on. The second version is a printed version of the document or form as it would normally appear. After printing these copies, the document or form is implemented at a sample of field or regional offices in the organization.

Choose the location where you are going to test the document. Then distribute the document and decide how long the test should run. Beta tests usually run for a specified period of time. You will also want to interview staff who distributed or used the document.

4.2 Informal methods

The best tests are those that include actual readers of the document. However, sometimes that is not possible. In these cases, more informal tests can be used. These informal tests do not account for the skills and needs of your readers. They can, however, give you an early indication of potential problems with the documents.

One simple and inexpensive method is to read the document aloud. You can also give the document to colleagues and ask them to read it. Having someone else read the document highlights areas that are not clear or problems with getting the message across.

Many computer software packages can also be used to evaluate written material. Two that are available are RightWriter and Grammatik. These software packages evaluate your writing for clarity. People who use them regularly say that over time their writing does become clearer.

However, just because a document is written at a grade eight reading level does not mean that it is easy to understand. The organization and design can still make the document difficult to read and use.

There are several standard readability tests that can give you a rough estimate of the level of education needed to read a document. A readability test can help you assess a piece of writing – but use it as only **one part** of your assessment.

Despite their limitations, readability tests can be useful in demonstrating a point. Consider the characteristics of your audience and then do a test of some of the documents that your department produces. Are they written at a grade level that is appropriate for your audience? On this page and the next are the instructions for one readability test – the Fry readability formula.

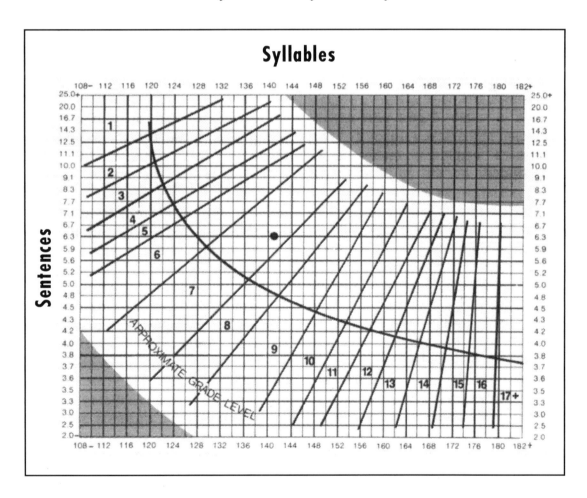

4.3 The Fry Readability Graph

The graph on the previous page gives you an estimate of the grade level of education that a reader needs to read the text with ease. You can apply the Fry readability graph to a text with as few as 100 words. To apply it to longer texts, just take three or more samples and average the results.

To find the reading level of material:

1. Randomly select three sample passages and count out exactly 100 words each, beginning with the beginning of a sentence. A word is defined as a group of symbols with a space on either side, for example, Joe, IRA, 1945 and &.

2. Count the number of sentences in each 100-word passage, estimating the length of the last sentence as a fraction to the nearest 1/10th.

3. Count the total number of syllables in each 100-word passage. Generally, there are as many syllables as vowel sounds. For example, "stop" is one syllable and "wanted" is two syllables. When counting syllables for numbers or acronyms, count one syllable for each symbol; for example, 1945 is four syllables. IRA is three syllables and & is one syllable. If you don't have a hand counter available, put a mark above every syllable in each word and then count the number of marks.

4. On the graph, plot the average sentence length for the three passages and join them with a line. Plot the average number of syllables for the three passages and join them with a line. Find where the two lines meet. The area where they meet gives you the approximate grade level a reader must have to understand the passage.

Adapted from material written by Edward Fry
May be reprinted without permission

Readability tests cannot tell you:
- how complex the ideas are;
- how well or poorly the material is written;
- whether the grammar is correct;
- whether the vocabulary and tone are appropriate for the intended audience;
- whether there is discriminatory language;
- whether there is gender, class, racial or cultural bias;
- whether information is presented in a sequence that makes sense to the reader;
- whether readers can find the information they need; or
- whether the design makes the document inviting and easy to read.

A simple way to get feedback from the public is to give the document to some members of the intended audience or to groups that represent the user and ask them what they think.

These informal testing methods are easy to do and cost very little money. They can be very useful when beginning to use plain language and can help you make sure the message is clear and understood by the intended audience.

5. WHAT TO DO WITH THE TEST RESULTS

Document testing gives you valuable information about how to improve the document. Always plan on more revisions after the testing. Few, if any, documents go through a test without requiring some further revisions. After analyzing the test results, you and your colleagues need to decide what revisions still need to be made. If there are major changes at this stage, it may be necessary to retest after the revisions are completed.

EXERCISE

TESTING AND REVISING THE DOCUMENT FOR USABILITY AND READABILITY

Use documents from the participants' program area or other appropriate documents.

Working in small groups, ask participants to develop and conduct a test of a document. Specifically, they should develop the variables they want to measure, and how to best test the document. Then, they should conduct the test. (Although there are limits in the classroom, this can be done effectively for focus group testing and scenario testing as well as questionnaire development.) Have participants discuss how they would revise the documents based on the test results.

MODULE 9

PUTTING IT ALL TOGETHER: WORKING WITH PLAIN LANGUAGE

Overview

The purpose of this module is to let participants work through the plain language process. This module allows participants to bring together what they have learned. It is also helpful to see the whole process from "beginning to end."

Objectives

This module reinforces what participants have learned by helping them integrate the various steps in the plain language process. By working through the entire process, participants will get a clearer picture of how to use the plain language techniques they have learned and how plain language results in effective and efficient communication.

Organization

This module is organized into the following sections:
- Task 1: Analyzing the audience
- Task 2: Writing for the reader
- Task 3: Getting feedback

Putting It All Together

This module is presented as one big exercise. It reinforces what participants have learned by helping them integrate the various steps in the plain language process. It would be useful to review the basic principles of the course before proceeding with the exercise.

Have participants create their own documents based on the scenarios at the end of this module or have them use documents from their program areas.

You will need a minimum of 2.5 hours for this exercise and preferably 3 to 4 hours. This exercise is easier if you can do your writing and revising on computers. You can either have small groups work on different parts of a document or have each group work on a different document.

The tasks below are based on the steps of the plain language process and are only a summary of the key points raised in the earlier modules. Have participants complete each task in the following order as they create their document. The Plain Language Checklist that is provided in this guide can also be used to help participants follow the plain language process.

Task 1:   **Analyzing the audience**

Focus on the audience for the document. Who will read it? Why will they read it?

TIP

This module works very well for the last one-half day of a longer course. However, don't attempt to do it if you do not have sufficient time.

Task 2:   **Writing for the reader**

- **Organization.** Make sure that the document is organized clearly and logically.

- **Words.** Check for unfamiliar or unclear words and for technical terms that are not defined.

- **Sentences.** Review the sentences for length and clarity. Decide where lists are necessary and check for passive voice.

- **Paragraphs.** Review the purpose and structure of each paragraph to make sure that they develop each topic clearly. Check the use of transition words.

- **Presenting your message effectively.** Make sure that the type size, type style and page format of the document are inviting and conducive to easy reading. Remember that a 12-point type size is a good average size to use.

Task 3:   **Getting feedback**

- **Testing.** Read the document aloud or give it to someone else to read. Test it on a readability graph or with a software package to give you an idea of revisions you may need to make before testing. Then decide which method you think is best if you were testing the document with readers.

- **Revisions based on the feedback.** Make any necessary revisions based on the feedback from others or the results of the readability or software testing.

MODULE 9   EXERCISE #1

EXERCISE

PUTTING IT ALL TOGETHER: WORKING WITH PLAIN LANGUAGE

Choose one of the following scenarios for this exercise. Have the participants, working individually or in groups:

1. Write a memo from directors to line staff. Budget cuts have made it necessary to reduce staff and services offered by their department. The memo should explain the reasons for the cutbacks and contain the criteria for determining which programs are to be scaled back and who may have to be laid off.

2. Write a letter from the Federal Business Development Bank to a group that has requested a start-up loan. They intend to create a firm to produce, market and export computer software for electric automobiles. The request for a loan has been denied. The letter should contain the reasons for the denial.

3. Write a briefing note to the Assistant Deputy Minister. The briefing note should detail the achievements up to today of their department's programs during the current fiscal year and also what remains to be accomplished. It can also include suggested changes to programs that have not met their goals.

PLAIN LANGUAGE CHECKLIST

Audience checklist

1. Who are my readers? What do they know about this subject?

2. Why will they read this document? What do my readers need to know about this subject?

Organization checklist

1. Have I presented information logically and in a way that makes sense to my readers?

2. Can my readers put my document into context? Do they understand what they are about to read, how the document is organized and what its purpose is?

3. Have I put the most important information first?

4. Can my readers quickly and easily find what they are looking for? Have I guided them through the text?

5. Have I used headings and subheadings that are:
   - descriptive of the text that follows,
   - consistent in style and design, and
   - logical and explicit?

Words checklist

1. Have I written directly to my readers?

2. What words would my readers use when talking about this subject?

3. What terms are familiar to me but likely to be unfamiliar to my readers?

4. Have I explained unfamiliar terms and acronyms?

5. Have I used:
   - verbs to describe action,
   - words that my readers know in ways that are familiar to them,
   - words with clear meanings,
   - appropriate examples, and
   - language that is free of bias?

6. Have I avoided using:
   - nominalizations,
   - jargon, and
   - words from foreign languages?

7. Have I used the words "may," "can" and "shall" correctly?

Sentence checklist

1. Have I written sentences with:
   - an average length of 15 to 25 words, and
   - only one idea?

2. Have I used active voice rather than passive voice?

3. Have I written clearly and concisely, without surplus words?

4. Have I kept the core of my sentences together?

5. Have I avoided using:
   - unnecessary preambles,
   - double negatives, and
   - prepositional phrases?

6. Have I used point form and tabulation lists that:
   - help to explain complex material or describe a sequence of steps to follow, and
   - are consistent in form and style?

Paragraph checklist

1. Have I used paragraphs with:
   - only one topic,
   - sentences that relate logically to the subject,
   - familiar material introducing new information, and
   - appropriate transitions?

Design checklist

1. Have I used:
   - a serif typeface, and
   - a type size of 10 or 12 points?

2. Do my headings and subheadings stand out?

3. In my headings and subheadings, have I used:
   - a type style that is different from the text,
   - various type sizes,
   - upper and lower case letters, and
   - one-line headings?

4. Have I used:
   - plenty of space between lines of type,
   - a justified left margin,
   - a ragged or unjustified right margin, and
   - plenty of white space on the page?

5. Have I used visual images appropriately?

Testing checklist

1. Have I decided what variables I am testing for?

2. Have I analyzed my audience? Do I know how many different "audiences" there are with whom I am going to test the document?

3. How many people should I include in the test groups?

4. What method should I use to test the document? Focus group testing? Scenario testing? Field surveys? Site testing?

5. What location will I use for the test?

6. How much will formal testing cost? How much time will it take?

7. If testing informally, whom will I choose to read my document?

8. Can I use RightWriter, Grammatik or a readability test to evaluate my document?

9. How will I evaluate the results of the testing?

10. What changes will I make to the document as a result of the testing?

11. Will I test the revised document?

COURSE OBJECTIVES

- Increase awareness of the benefits of plain language.

- Increase understanding of plain language techniques.

- Develop skills for using plain language.

INTRODUCING PLAIN LANGUAGE

- What is plain language?

- Where did the term "plain language" come from?

- Plain language in the federal government.

- Why do written communications break down?

- The plain language process.

WHAT IS PLAIN LANGUAGE?

- An approach to communication.
    - effective communications
    - efficient communications

- An attitude toward the reader.
    - respect the reader
    - understand the reader's purpose
    - empathize with the reader's needs

- A process; not a set of rules.

PLAIN LANGUAGE:

- Organizes information so that it makes sense to the reader.

- Speaks directly to the reader.

- Matches the vocabulary and style of writing to the needs of the reader.

- Explains technical terms and uses examples that relate to the reader's experience.

- Uses concrete words with common meanings.

- Uses layout and design appropriate to the content of the document and the needs of the reader.

PLAIN LANGUAGE IS <u>NOT</u>:

- Simple-minded writing.

- Dick-and-Jane vocabulary.

- Condescending or writing down to the reader.

- The misuse of language.

- The inaccurate representation of professional or technical or legal language.

WHY PLAIN LANGUAGE?

- Unclear messages waste time and cause confusion.

- Readers have different reading skills.

- The public has difficulty understanding government documents.

BENEFITS OF PLAIN LANGUAGE

Plain language:

- Helps all readers understand information.

- Avoids misunderstandings and errors.

- Saves time for both you and your readers.

- Reaches people who cannot read well.

BENEFITS OF PLAIN LANGUAGE

- The Ministry of Colleges and Universities redesigned the application for the Ontario Student Assistance Program. The new application takes 50% less time to process. As a result, the program has been able to accomplish other work and improve customer service to students because of the staff time saved in processing the forms.

- The Ontario Human Rights Commission used to hand out copies of the Ontario Human Rights Code when anyone asked how to make a complaint. Then they produced plain language documents about the complaints process and basic information about the Human Rights Code. They estimate that they now save $15,000 per year in printing costs alone.

BENEFITS OF PLAIN LANGUAGE

United Kingdom:

- Customs and Excise used a form that had an error rate of 55%. Redesigning the form reduced the error rate to 3%, saving staff 3,700 hours in processing time. It cost the Department about $3,000 to rewrite the form, but saved about $38,700 a year in processing costs.

- The Department of Defence redesigned an internal expense claim form. The new form cost about $15,000 to produce, but saved 80,000 staff hours or about $475,000 a year.

- The Property Service Agency improved the design of a contract and saved about $190,000 a year.

- In 1984, a plain English application form for legal aid was introduced. The form cost about $50,500 to develop and test, but saved about $2.9 million in staff time each year.

BENEFITS OF PLAIN LANGUAGE

- The Lotteries Branch of the Ministry of Consumer and Commercial Relations issued a bulletin that resulted in 20 telephone calls per day. They wrote a memo in plain language to clarify the bulletin and the calls stopped. If each call consumed five minutes of staff time, the Branch was able to save 1 hour and 40 minutes per day (or more than 300 hours per year) as a result of this effort. This time can now be spent on other activities.

WHY DO WRITTEN COMMUNICATIONS BREAK DOWN?

The Communication Process

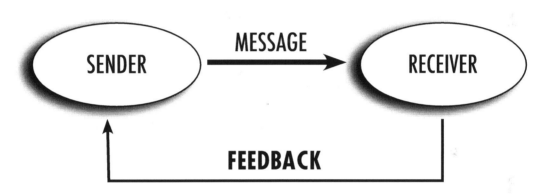

THE PLAIN LANGUAGE PROCESS

1. Understand your readers' needs.

2. Create a message that matches your needs with the needs of your readers.

3. Get feedback to make sure your message is effective.

THE STARTING POINT: YOUR READER AND YOUR PURPOSE

- The readers of a document.

- The purpose of a document.

- The impact of a document.

"Communication equals remembering what it's like not to understand."

Richard Saul Wurman
Information Anxiety

THE BUILDING BLOCKS OF PLAIN LANGUAGE WRITING

Before you begin writing, ask yourself these questions.

1. Who is your audience?

2. Why are you writing this document?

3. What do you want your reader to do?

THE PURPOSE OF A DOCUMENT

- Report

- Ask

- Inform

- Influence

- Explain

THE IMPACT OF A DOCUMENT

Is the reader supposed to:

- do something?

- learn something?

- learn to do something?

- change their point of view?

- keep the document for future reference?

PRINCIPLES OF ORGANIZATION

- Organize the information logically.

- Orient your reader to the text.

- Put the most important information first.

- Help your readers find information.

- Put all the information about a specific subject in one place.

USING APPROPRIATE WORDS

- Make your writing personal.

- Use words with clear meanings.

- Use words your reader will understand.

- Use verbs rather than nouns.

- Avoid or explain technical terms.

- Avoid chains of nouns.

USING APPROPRIATE WORDS

- Avoid using acronyms.

- Avoid using jargon.

- Avoid using words from foreign languages.

- Use " may" and "can" correctly.

- Use "shall" correctly.

- Avoid gender reference, stereotypes and biased language.

A GOOD EXAMPLE OF MAKING YOUR WRITING PERSONAL

If You Suspect Sexual Abuse

The best way to respond to a child who you suspect may have been sexually abused is to listen carefully to what the child says and to be attentive to his or her behaviour. Show your concern. Ask if anything is the matter. But do not press for an answer. Let the child know that you are ready to listen at any time.

USE WORDS WITH CLEAR MEANINGS

"The employee coordinates selected horizontal administrative activities and acts as a functional coordinator for cross-sectoral development initiatives…"

(ad for Senior Project Officer position)

USE WORDS YOUR READER WILL UNDERSTAND

Instead of:	Use:
accomplish	do
ascertain	find out
disseminate	send out, distribute
endeavour	try
expedite	hasten, speed up
facilitate	work out, devise, form
in lieu of	instead of
locality	place
optimum	best, greatest, most
strategize	plan
utilize	use

USE VERBS RATHER THAN NOUNS

Original:

Establishment of goals for the hiring, training and promotion of designated group employees. Such goals will consider projections for hiring, promotions, terminations, lay-offs, recalls, retirements and, where possible, the projected availability of qualified designated group members.

Revised:

Establish goals for hiring, training and promoting employees from designated groups. Such goals will reflect the rate at which we will hire, promote, terminate, lay off or recall members of designated groups and the rate at which they will retire. Where possible, the goals will project how many qualified members will be available.

AVOID OR EXPLAIN TECHNICAL TERMS

Original:

Spousal registered retirement income fund – A spousal RRIF is an RRIF under which your spouse is the annuitant that has received funds from a spousal RRSP or another spousal RRIF.

Revised:

A spousal registered retirement income fund is a reserve which pays yearly to your spouse and which has received money from a spousal RRSP or another spousal RRIF.

AVOID CHAINS OF NOUNS

- Objective human resources management system.

- Proposed project expenditure levels.

- Human-related fish kills.

- Sound long-range accommodation planning process.

- Government post-contract financial audit coverage.

- Explosion relief provisions.

AVOID CHAINS OF NOUNS

"Better Beginnings is a 25-year interministerial/intergovernmental longitudinal prevention policy research demonstration project."

AVOID USING ACRONYMS

Original:

> A DNA sex probe was developed at DFO's PBS, W. Vancouver Laboratory, in conjunction with Sea Spring Salmon Farm and the Science Council of B.C.

Revised:

> A DNA sex probe was developed at the Department of Fisheries and Ocean's Pacific Biological Station, West Vancouver Laboratory, in conjunction with Sea Spring Salmon Farm and the Science Council of British Columbia.

AVOID USING JARGON

- Level playing field.

- Downtime.

- Leading edge.

- Streamline.

- Interface with.

- Rationalization of resources.

AVOID USING WORDS FROM FOREIGN LANGUAGES

- e.g.

- i.e.

- per annum

- n.b.

USE "MAY" AND "CAN" CORRECTLY

- "May"
  - Conditional choice
  - Permission

- "Can"
  - Ability
  - Permission

TRANSPARENCY #13   MODULE 4

USE "SHALL" CORRECTLY

- Obligation
  - "Must"

- Future tense
  - "Will"

WRITING CLEAR AND EFFECTIVE SENTENCES

- Active voice.

- Positive tone.

- One idea to a sentence.

- Clear, direct and short sentences.

- Reduce the filler.

- Use adverbs and adjectives sparingly.

WRITING CLEAR AND EFFECTIVE SENTENCES

- Avoid unnecessary preambles.

- Eliminate double negatives.

- Eliminate prepositional phrases.

- Place modifiers correctly.

- Put parallel ideas in parallel constructions.

- Use point form and lists appropriately.

WRITE IN THE ACTIVE VOICE

Original:

Citizenship cannot be renounced merely by making a personal declaration to this effect.

Revised:

You cannot renounce your citizenship merely by making a personal declaration.

WRITE IN THE ACTIVE VOICE

Original:

The police look for facts that prove a crime occurred and that can be used as evidence in court. If there is sufficient evidence, and the alleged offender can be located, criminal charges can be laid.

Revised:

The police look for facts that prove a crime occurred and that the crown attorney can use as evidence in court. If there is sufficient evidence, and the police can locate the alleged offender, they can lay criminal charges.

A GOOD EXAMPLE OF ACTIVE VOICE

Employers pay their workers every week, every two weeks or once a month. You can be paid in cash, by cheque or by direct deposit to your bank account. Your pay stub shows how much you earned. It also lists deductions for taxes, pension, unemployment insurance and any other items that are deducted from your pay.

ONE IDEA TO A SENTENCE

Original:

Some commercial sources such as secondhand bookstores, book exchanges or book banks, and book fairs featuring used books recycle previously purchased books and do not create new sales for the industry.

Revised:

Some commercial sources such as secondhand bookstores, book exchanges or book banks, and book fairs featuring used books recycle previously purchased books. They do not create new sales for the industry.

ONE IDEA TO A SENTENCE

Original:

All travellers, including children, may be eligible for certain exemptions and as each traveller must also meet the entry requirements of several government agencies, it will be necessary for each person to complete a card.

Revised:

All travellers, including children, must meet the entry requirements of several government agencies. Also, you may be eligible for certain exemptions. For these reasons, each person must complete a card.

WRITE CLEAR, DIRECT AND SHORT SENTENCES

Original:

And now with new Canadian standards for rating windows as well as incentive programs in certain provinces for consumers and builders using high-performance varieties, some manufacturers are working to bring their products up to the performance levels needed to qualify under the incentive programs.

Revised:

Some window manufacturers are working to improve their products because of new Canadian standards for rating windows and new incentive programs adopted by certain provinces. Consumers and builders will qualify for these programs if they use high-performance varieties.

AN EXAMPLE THAT USES SHORT SENTENCES TO MAKE ITS POINT

The solution is simple. Don't take things that don't belong to you. Before you buy or borrow something from a friend, make sure that it's theirs to sell or lend. If your friends are involved in theft or break and enter, try to talk them out of it. If you can't, leave the scene, because you can also be charged.

AN EXAMPLE OF THE GOOD USE OF TABULATION

Your representatives are your link to government.

They can:

- represent your ideas when arguing for or against a proposed law,

- ask questions about the government on your behalf,

- present important issues,

- help you if you need services from government,

- help you find the right government or department to contact, and

- help you if you have a problem with any government.

KEEP THE SENTENCE CORE TOGETHER

Original:

> **Our records indicate that** on the date shown on the address label on the reverse side of this questionnaire, **you either completed this course or for some other reason, left the course early**.

Revised:

> A date appears on the address label on the reverse side of this questionnaire. Our records indicate you either completed the course or left the course early on that date.

USE ADVERBS AND ADJECTIVES SPARINGLY

- Definite decision.
- Mutually agreed.
- Final deadline.
- True facts.
- Enclosed inside.
- Absolutely essential.
- Grave emergency.
- Acute crisis.
- Honest opinion.
- Positive benefits.
- New innovation.

AVOID UNNECESSARY PREAMBLES

- "It is important to add that…"

- "It is interesting to note that…"

- "It may be recalled that…"

- "Despite the fact that…"

- "Clear beyond dispute is the fact that…"

- "There are…"

- "It is…"

ELIMINATE DOUBLE NEGATIVES

- "He was not absent."

- "The procedure will not be ineffective."

- "It was never illegitimate."

ELIMINATE PREPOSITIONAL PHRASES

Instead of:	Use:
with regard to	about
by means of	by
in the event that	if
until such time	until
in accordance with	by, under
in view of the fact	because

PLACING MODIFIERS CORRECTLY

Original:

My client has discussed your proposal to fill the drainage ditch with his partners.

Revised:

My client has discussed with his partners your proposal to fill the drainage ditch.

PUT PARALLEL IDEAS IN PARALLEL CONSTRUCTION

Original:

Going on vacation…

- **Inform** a neighbour of your departure…
- **Have** your neighbour pick up newspapers…
- **Small** valuables should be stored…
- **Use** clock timers that activate lights…
- **Before** leaving, ensure all entries are secured…

Revised:

Going on vacation…

- **Inform** a neighbour of your departure…
- **Have** your neighbour pick up newspapers…
- **Store** small valuables…
- **Use** clock timers that activate lights…
- **Secure** all entries before leaving…

WRITING CLEAR AND EFFECTIVE PARAGRAPHS

- The purpose of the paragraph.

- The structure of the paragraph.

- The use of transitions.

CLEAR AND SIMPLE PARAGRAPHS

"The groups and organizations on the following pages are community partners in literacy. Some have a long-standing involvement in literacy; others are relatively new to the issue. Literacy is benefiting from the experience of all these groups. They bring a strong tradition of commitment and service. Voluntary literacy groups in Canada have long played a critical role in the effort to make this a fully literate country. Groups without a specific 'literacy' focus are in an excellent position to incorporate the literacy needs of their clients into their programs. They help to ensure that more people who need help to improve their reading and writing skills can be reached."

Partners in Literacy, p. 13

CHAINING IDEAS

Very often we, in government and administration, have to set up new categories. Only certain people in a category can receive assistance. We don't have a special word for this category; so what we do is decide that we will take an everyday word and give it special meaning. We salve our conscience by saying, "Oh, I've put it in the definitions section so people ought to refer to it there." We ignore the fact that many readers don't know about definitions sections and are not used to using them. We also ignore the fact that we place a great psychological strain on readers; we define a word in the beginning of the text and then expect them to remember its special use through 170-odd pages.

WAYS TO ORGANIZE A PARAGRAPH

- Cause, then effect.
- Chronology.
- Facts, then opinion.
- General, then particular situation.
- Precedent, then application.
- Proposal, then response.
- Question, then answer.
- Requirement, then justification.
- Rule, then exceptions.

TRANSITION WORDS

- Similarity
- Contrast
- Cause
- Sequence
- Conclusion

PRESENTING YOUR MESSAGE EFFECTIVELY

- Text and readability.

- Page format.

- Headings and subheadings.

- Highlighting.

- Table of contents.

- Visual effectiveness.

TYPE STYLE

- Serif

    Times New Roman

    Garamond

    Palatino

- Sans Serif

    Univers

    Arial

TEXT IN ALL CAPS IS HARD TO READ

TEXT SET IN ALL-CAPITALS IS HARDER TO READ THAN TEXT SET IN UPPER AND LOWER CASE. RESEARCHERS HAVE FOUND THAT PEOPLE READ CONTINUOUS CAPITAL LETTERS AT A SLOWER RATE THAN SMALL LETTERS.

RIGHT JUSTIFICATION IS HARDER TO READ

RIGHT JUSTIFICATION

Technology, like international competition and the emergence of an integrated world economy, is changing the way Canadians work. Computers are familiar pieces of equipment in offices and factories, and Canadians working on the shop floor and in the boardroom are having to learn new tasks. The new workplace skills require more education, more training, better communication and higher levels of literacy. Skilled minds are taking over from the skilled hands of yesteryear.

RAGGED RIGHT MARGIN

Technology, like international competition and the emergence of an integrated world economy, is changing the way Canadians work. Computers are familiar pieces of equipment in offices and factories, and Canadians working on the shop floor and in the boardroom are having to learn new tasks. The new workplace skills require more education, more training, better communication and higher levels of literacy. Skilled minds are taking over from the skilled hands of yesteryear.

HIGHLIGHTING

- Boxes

- Boldface

- Bullets

- Italic print

- Underlining

- Colour

TESTING AND REVISING FOR USABILITY AND READABILITY

- What is document testing?

- Why test and when to do it?

- How to test a document for usability and readability.

- What to do with the test results.

TESTING
Check with the experts – your readers

Formal Tests

- Focus Group Testing.
- Scenario Testing.
- Field Surveys.
- Site Testing.

Informal Tests

- Read your document aloud.
- Ask someone else to read your draft.
- Use computer software to check grammar and style.
- Do a readability test.

FOCUS GROUPS

Advantages

- Easy to organize.
- Useful for subjective measures.

Disadvantages

- Not appropriate for comprehension or usability.
- Depends on quality of group leader.

SCENARIO TESTING

Advantages

- Excellent for comprehension and usability.
- Material tested in simulated context.

Disadvantages

- Time-consuming.
- Scenario must be simple.

SURVEYS

Advantages

- Easy to administer.
- Can use larger sample.

Disadvantages

- Takes time to develop questionnaire.
- Response rate can be low.
- Don't get to see reader in action.

SITE TESTS

Advantages

- Real time, real experience.
- Can test both user and operational characteristics.

Disadvantages

- Risk in changing operations.
- Must test for enough time to assess results.
- Cumbersome if done in parallel.

CONDUCTING THE TEST

- Choose variables.

- Choose sample.

- Choose appropriate method.

- Conduct test.

- Analyze results.

- Use results to revise document.

READABILITY TESTS CANNOT TELL YOU:

- How complex the ideas are.
- How well or poorly the material is written.
- Whether the grammar is correct.
- Whether vocabulary and tone are appropriate for the intended audience.
- Whether there is discriminatory language.
- Whether there is gender, class, racial or cultural bias.
- Whether information is presented in a sequence that makes sense to the reader.
- Whether readers can find the information they need.
- Whether the design makes the document inviting and easy to read.

TESTING ISSUES

- Time

    "We don't have time to test."

    "This document has to be at the printer next week."

- Money

    "We don't have the budget."

DERIVATIVE NOUNS AND VERB EQUIVALENTS

Derivative noun	Verb form
acceptance	accept
application	apply
approval	approve
assumption	assume
calculation	calculate
certification	certify
complaint	complain
conservation	conserve
consideration	consider
contribution	contribute
decision	decide
deduction	deduct
delivery	deliver
designation	designate (name, appoint)
deterioration	deteriorate
determination	determine
disclosure	disclose
discovery	discover
disposal, disposition	dispose (sell, give away)
distribution	distribute
education	educate
enforcement	enforce
examination	examine
filing	file
inclusion	include
information	inform
investigation	investigate
movement	move
objection	object
payment	pay
persistence	persist
prevention	prevent
promotion	promote
qualification	qualify
reaction	react
receipt	receive
recurrence	recur
reduction	reduce
reliance	rely
remittance	remit
residence	reside
resistance	resist
specification	specify
statement	state
submission	submit

PLAIN LANGUAGE CLEAR AND SIMPLE

TRANSITION WORDS

Similarity

again
also
and
as a matter of fact
as well
besides
for example
for instance
furthermore
in addition
in other words
in particular
indeed
moreover
namely
similarly
specifically
that is

Contrast

although
but
conversely
despite this
however
instead
nevertheless
on the contrary
still
yet

Sequence

afterwards
at last
at length
at the same time
eventually

Cause

as a result
accordingly
because
consequently
for
hence
if…then
since
so
thus

Conclusion

in conclusion
in short
in summary
on the whole
to summarize
finally
first, next, last
immediately
later
meanwhile
next
presently
previously
since
soon
subsequently
then
while

PREPOSITIONAL PHRASES AND REPLACEMENTS

Prepositional phrases	Replace with
at this (that) point in time	now (then)
as a consequence of	because of
by means of	by, under
by reason of	because of
by virtue of	by, under
for the purpose of	to
for the reason that	because
from the point of view of	from, for
in accordance with	by, under
in addition to	besides
inasmuch as	since
in association with	with
in case of	if
in connection with	with, about, concerning
in excess of	more than, over
in favour of	for
in order to	to
in relation to	about, concerning
insofar as	since
in the absence of	without
in the course of	during
in the event of/that	if
in the nature of	like
in the neighbourhood of	near
in the vicinity of	near
in view of	because of
on a daily basis	daily
on a regular basis	regularly
on the grounds of	because of
prior to	before
subsequent to	after
until such time as	until
with the exception of	except
with reference to	about, concerning
with regard to	about, concerning
with respect to	about, for, on

PLAIN LANGUAGE **CLEAR** AND **SIMPLE**

SUBSTITUTES FOR MULTI-SYLLABLE WORDS

Instead of: Use:

accomplish	do
ascertain	find out
disseminate	send out, distribute
endeavour	try
expedite	hasten, speed up
facilitate	work out, devise, form
in lieu of	instead of
locality	place
optimum	best, greatest, most
strategize	plan
utilize	use

GUIDELINES FOR TABULATION

1. The items in the list must form a logical group. Avoid making a list of (a) bread, (b) eggs and (c) the prime minister.

2. Each item should contain only one idea.

3. All items in the list should be in the same form. Avoid beginning some items with a noun and others with a verb. Avoid varying the tenses of the verbs you use in a list.

4. Each item should work separately with the lead-in to form a complete sentence. Concluding material must fit in too, if the sentence continues after the last item on the list.

5. Put anything common to all items in the lead-in. The lead-in is the text before the bullets. The text after the bullets is the list.

6. The list should be indented to set it apart from the lead-in and any concluding material. Return to the left margin for any statement following the list.

7. Use bullets to identify each item in the list. Use numbers instead of bullets only when you are describing step-by-step procedures. Avoid using both numbers and bullets in a list.

8. If bullets are being used, all items in the list should begin with a lower case letter.

9. When items contain commas or are lengthy, use semicolons at the end of each item. Otherwise use commas or no punctuation. Put a period after the last item if it is the end of the sentence.

10. If the list consists of alternatives, put "or" after the second last item. If the list is inclusive, put "and" after the second last item.

REFERENCES

General

American Institutes for Research, Document Design Centre. 1979. *Simplifying Documents*. Washington, D.C.: American Institutes for Research, Document Design Center.

Baldwin, Ruth. 1990. *Clear Writing and Literacy*. Toronto: Ontario Literacy Coalition.

Benson, Robert W. 1984/1985. "The End of Legalese: The Game is Over." *New York University Review of Law and Social Change*. Vol. 13, 519–573

Berger, Thomas R. 1989. "Law, the Charter and the Idea of Canada." *Law vs. Learning*. Toronto: Canadian Law Information Council.

Block, Gertrude. 1986. *Effective Legal Writing*. Third Edition. Mineola, New York: Foundation.

Breen, Mary and Janis Wood Catano. 1987. *Checklist for Evaluating Health Education Materials*. Toronto: Metropolitan Movement for Literacy.

Calamai, Peter. 1987. *Broken Words: Why Five Million Canadians Are Illiterate*. Toronto: Southam Newspaper Group.

Canadian Bar Association and Canadian Bankers' Association. 1990. *The Decline and Fall of Gobbledygook: Report on Plain Language Documentation*. Ottawa: Canadian Bar Association.

Canadian Legal Information Centre's Plain Language Centre. 1989. *Plain Language Overview: Income Tax Guide and Income Tax Return*. Unpublished Paper.

Charrow, Veda R., and Myra K. Erhardt. 1986. *Clear and Effective Legal Writing.* Boston, Toronto: Little Brown & Co.

Charrow, Veda R. 1982. *Language in the Bureaucracy.* New York: Ablex Publishing.

Child, Barbara. 1988. *Drafting Legal Documents: Materials and Problems.* St. Paul, Minn.: West Publishing Co.

Coe, Richard M. 1990. *Process, Form and Substances: A Rhetoric for Advanced Writers.* Englewood Cliffs, N.J.: Prentice Hall.

Dick, Robert C. 1985. *Legal Drafting.* Toronto: Carswell.

Duffy, Thomas. 1985. *Readability Formulas: What is the Use?* Technical Report Number 23. Pittsburgh: Communications Design Center.

Eagleson, Robert D. 1988. "Efficiency in Legal Drafting." *Adelaide Law Review,* 1–41.

Eagleson, Robert D. 1989. *The Case for Plain Language.* Address at Osgoode Hall. July 15, 1988. Toronto. Canadian Law Information Centre.

Eagleson, Robert D. 1990. *Writing in Plain English.* Canberra: Australian Government Publishing Service.

Elbow, Peter. 1981. *Writing With Power.* Don Mills, Ontario: Oxford University Press.

Felker, Daniel, et al. November 1981. *Guidelines for Document Designers.* Washington, D.C.: American Institutes for Research, Document Design Center.

Felsenfeld, Carl, and Alan Siegel. 1981. *Writing Contracts in Plain English.* St. Paul, Minn.: West Publishing Co.

Fisher, Phil, and David Sless. 1989. *Improving Information Management in the Insurance Industry.* Occasional Papers No. 10. Canberra: Communication Research Institute of Australia.

Flesch, Rudolf. 1979. *The ABC of Style.* New York: Collier Books.

Garner, Bryan A. 1991. *The Elements of Legal Style.* New York: Oxford University Press.

Goldfarb, Ronald L., and James C. Raymond. 1982. *Clear Understanding: A Legal Guide to Writing.* New York: Random House.

Gopen, George D. 1981. *Writing from a Legal Perspective.* St. Paul, Minn.: West Publishing Co.

Gopen, George D. November 1987. "The State of Legal Writing: Res Ipsa Loquitur." *Michigan Law Review.* Vol. 86, No. 333.

Gowers, Sir Ernest. 1987. *The Complete Plain Words.* Harmondsworth: Penguin Books.

Kelsey, Judith. 1988. *I Am Worth the Effort.* St. John's, Newfoundland: Iris Kirby House (St. John's Transition House).

Kimble, Joseph. 1992. *Plain English: A Charter for Clear Writing.* Michigan: Thomas M. Cooley Law Review, Volume 9, Number 1.

King, Ruth. 1991. *Talking Gender: A Guide to Nonsexist Communication.* Toronto: Copp Clark Pitman.

Klauser, Henriette Anne. 1986. *Writing on Both Sides of the Brain.* San Francisco: Harper and Row.

Larocque, Greg, Heidemarie MacLean, and William Marshall. 1988. *Administrative Writing: Memos & Letters*. Ottawa: Public Service Commission of Canada, Training Programs Branch.

Lefrere, Paul. 1981. "The Impact and Implications of the New Communications Technology." *Information Design Journal*. Vol. 2, 91–96.

Maggio, Rosalie. 1987. *The Non-Sexist Word Finding: A Dictionary of Gender-Free Usage*. New York: Oryx Press.

Moore, Michael D., Walter S. Avis, and Jim W. Corder. 1983. *Handbook of Current English, Second Canadian Edition*. Toronto: Gage Publishing.

Morehead, Alison, and Robyn Penman. 1989. *Federal Government Information Campaigns: A Critical Review*. Occasional Papers No. 11. Canberra: Communication Research Institute of Australia.

Multiculturalism and Citizenship Canada. 1991. *Plain Language: Clear and Simple*. Ottawa: Minister of Supply and Services.

National Consumer Council. 1981. *Plain English Training Kit*. London: National Consumer Council.

Ontario Ministry of Education. 1991. *Implementing Plain Language: A Manager's Guide*. Toronto: Literacy Branch.

Perrin, Timothy. 1990. *Better Writing for Lawyers*. Toronto: Law Society of Upper Canada.

Ray, Mary B., and Jill J. Ramsfield. 1987. *Legal Writing: Getting It Right and Getting It Written*. St. Paul, Minn.: West Publishing Co.

Redish, Janice. 1979. *Readability*. Washington: AIR Document Design Center.

Roberts, Philip Davies. 1987. *Plain English: A User's Guide.* Harmondsworth: Penguin Books.

Rooke, Constance. 1991. *A Grammar Booklet for Lawyers.* Toronto: Law Society of Upper Canada.

Strunk, William Jr., and E.B. White. 1979. *The Elements of Style.* New York: Macmillan.

Suchan, James, and Robert Colucci. 1989. *An Analysis of Communication Efficiency Between High-Impact and Bureaucratic Written Communication.* Management Communication Quarterly, May 1989.

Suchan, James, and Robert Colucci. 1989. *The High Cost of Bureaucratic Written Communications.* Business Horizons, Volume 34, Number 2. Indianapolis: Indiana University Graduate School of Business.

Thompson, Edward T. 1988. *How to Write Clearly.* New York: International Paper Company.

U.S. Department of Commerce. 1984. *Plain English Works for Business: Twelve Case Studies.* Washington: Office of Consumer Affairs.

Westheimer, Patricia H. 1988. *The Perfect Memo.* Glenview, Illinois: Scott, Foresman and Company.

Wright, Patricia. 1980. *Textual Literacy: An Outline of Psychological Research on Reading and Writing.* New York: Plenum Publishing.

Wydick, Richard C. 1979. *Plain English for Lawyers.* Durham, North Carolina: Carolina Academic Press.

Zinsser, William. 1988. *On Writing Well.* New York: Harper and Row.

FORMS

Barnett, Robert. 1984. *The Form Designer's Quick Reference Guide.* Evatt, A.C.T.: Robert Barnett and Associates.

Barnett, Robert. 1988. *Cutting the Garbage: Designing Better Computer Input Forms.* Occasional Papers No. 2 (revised November 1988). Canberra: Communication Research Institute of Australia.

Barnett, Robert. 1988. *Forms for the General Public: Do They Really Work?* Occasional Papers No. 5 (revised 1989). Canberra: Communication Research Institute of Australia.

Barnett, Robert. 1988. *Managing Business Forms.* Canberra: Communication Research Institute of Australia.

Barnett, Robert, and David Sless. 1989. *Testing and Evaluating Forms.* Occasional Papers No. 9. Canberra: Communication Research Institute of Australia.

Caron, Steven C., et al. 1988. *Standard Business Forms and Agreements.* Ottawa: Proform Publishing.

Communication Research Institute of Australia. 1986. *Forms Data Sheets.* Canberra: Communication Research Institute of Australia.

Duffy, Thomas, et al. 1988. *Creating Usable Manuals and Forms: A Document Design Symposium.* Technical Report Series, Number 42. Pittsburgh: Communications Design Center, Carnegie Mellon.

Dykstra, Gail S. August 21, 1987. *Plain Language, Legal Documents and Forms: Background Information.* [Unpublished] Paper presented at Canadian Institute for the Administration of Justice Seminar on Legislative Drafting and Interpretation.

Foers, J.M. December 1986. *Forms Design: An International Perspective.* London: Inland Revenue.

Forms Information Centre. 1983. *Colour in Forms: A Brief Guide.* Reading: England: Forms Information Centre, Department of Typography and Graphics Communication, University of Reading.

Forms Information Centre. 1989. *Data Entry Boxes for Computer Input Forms.* Reading, England: Forms Information Centre, Department of Typography and Graphics Communication, University of Reading.

Forms Information Centre. 1984. *Forms Design: A Guide to Equipment and Materials.* Reading, England: Forms Information Centre, Department of Typography and Graphics Communication, University of Reading.

Forms Information Centre. 1984. *News Sheet 1: Language of Forms.* Reading, England: Forms Information Centre, Department of Typography and Graphics Communication, University of Reading.

Forms Information Centre. 1985. *News Sheet 2: Microcomputer Package for Forms Education.* Reading, England: Forms Information Centre, Department of Typography and Graphics Communication, University of Reading.

Forms Information Centre. 1986. *News Sheet 3: Comprehensibility of Coloured Printing.* Reading, England: Forms Information Centre, Department of Typography and Graphics Communication, University of Reading.

Forms Information Centre. 1986. *News Sheet 4: Dates as Answers on Forms.* Reading, England: Forms Information Centre, Department of Typography and Graphics Communication, University of Reading.

Forms Information Centre. 1988. *News Sheet 5: Size of Handwriting on Forms.* Reading, England: Forms Information Centre, Department of Typography and Graphics Communication, University of Reading.

Forms Information Centre. 1988. *News Sheet 6: Legibility of Condensed Letter Forms.* Reading, England: Forms Information Centre, Department of Typography and Graphics Communication, University of Reading.

Forms Information Centre. 1989. *News Sheet 10: Public Preferences for How Numbers Are Presented on Forms.* Reading, England: Forms Information Centre, Department of Typography and Graphics Communication, University of Reading.

Forms Information Centre. 1989. *News Sheet 11: Public Understanding of Relative Quantities.* Reading, England: Forms Information Centre, Department of Typography and Graphics Communication, University of Reading.

Forms Information Centre. 1989. *Topic Sheet 1: Legibility.* Reading, England: Forms Information Centre, Department of Typography and Graphics Communication, University of Reading.

Forms Information Centre. 1989. *Topic Sheet 2: Signature Space.* Reading, England: Forms Information Centre, Department of Typography and Graphics Communication, University of Reading.

Forms Information Centre. 1989. *Topic Sheet 3: Questions and Answers.* Reading, England: Forms Information Centre, Department of Typography and Graphics Communication, University of Reading.

Inland Revenue. 1984. *Forms: Making Them Work for You.* London: Mary Glasgow Publications.

Lewis, David. 1986. "The Cost of Errors on Forms." *Information Design Journal.* Vol. 4/3.

Magnus, S.W. 1988. *Butterworths Company Forms Manual.* London: Butterworths and Co.

Management Services Division of the Civil Services Department. 1972. *Design of Forms in Government Departments.* London: HMSO.

Sanderson, Stephen L.P., et al. 1987. *Camera Ready Forms.* Ottawa: Proform Publishing Ltd.

Sless, David. 1985. *Form Evaluation: Some Sample Methods.* Canberra: Department of Sport, Recreation and Tourism.

Wright, Patricia. 1981. "Informed Design on Forms." *Information Design Journal.* Vol. 2, Nos. 3 and 4.

Research

Bentley, Diana. 1984. *How and Why of Readability.* Reading, England: University of Reading.

Breen, Mary J., and Janis Wood Catano. 1987. *Can She Read It? Readability and Literacy in Health Education.* Toronto: Healthsharing.

Campbell, Leo J. 1982. *Understanding the Language of Public Documents Because Readability Formulas Don't.* New York: Ablex Publishing.

Charrow, Veda R., 1983. *A Study of the Comprehensibility of Automobile Recall Letters.* Washington: American Institutes for Research.

Coleman, E.B. 1962. "Improving Comprehensibility by Shortening Sentences." *Journal of Applied Psychology.* Vol. 46.

Duffy, Thomas, et al. 1985. *Designing Usable Texts.* Orlando, Fla.: Academic Press.

Klare, George. 1979. "Writing to Inform: Making it Readable." *Information Design Journal.* Vol. 1, No. 2.

Kolers, P. A. 1975. *Readability.* Toronto: Methuen.

"Medication Education. Roche's Commitment to Understanding." 1984. *Plain English Works: Twelve Case Studies.* Washington, D.C.: U.S. Department of Commerce.

Redish, Janice C., et al. 1981. "Evaluating the Effects of Document Design Principles." *Information Design Journal.* Vol. 2, Nos. 3 and 4.

Rose, Andrew M. 1981. "Problems in Public Documents." *Information Design Journal.* Vol. 2, Nos. 3 and 4.

Waller, Robert. "Designing a Government Form: A Case Study." *Information Design Journal.* Vol. 4, No. 1.

Walmsley, S.A., et al. 1981. "Effects of Document Simplification on the Reading Comprehension of the Elderly." *Journal of Reading Behaviour.* Vol. 8, No. 3.

Made in the USA
Middletown, DE
04 November 2017